Asking Styles

Asking Styles

Revolutionize Your Fundraising

Brian Saber

President, Asking Matters

Asking Styles: Revolutionize Your Fundraising

Published by Asking Matters™

Asking Matters
P.O. Box 1295
Maplewood, NJ 07040
www.askingmatters.com

This publication contains the opinions and ideas of the author. It is intended to provide helpful and informative material on the subject matter covered. It is sold with the understanding that the author and publisher are not engaged in rendering professional services in the book. If the reader requires personal assistance or advice, a competent professional should be consulted. The author and publisher specifically disclaim any responsibility for any liability, loss, or risk, personal or otherwise, which is incurred as a consequence, directly or indirectly, of the use and application of any of the contents of this book. No liability is assumed for damages resulting from the use of information contained within.

Printed in the United States of America

ISBN-10: 1720610282
ISBN-13: 978-1720610281

Cover designed by Thomas Edward West and Melina Furlong
Interior design by Thomas Edward West of Amarna Books and Media
Back cover photograph of Brian Saber by Colleen D'Alessandro
Interior photographs of Brian Saber by Yasmeen Anderson

contents

dedication

This book is dedicated to everyone in our glorious nonprofit sector who goes out to ask individuals for charitable gifts face-to-face.

For most of you this work isn't easy or fun, though it can be fascinating. Whether you ask as staff or volunteers, you ask because you care. You ask because you want the world to be a better place and you'll do what you can to make that so. You ask because giving back is in your DNA.

Chances are you don't ask because your dream was to be a fundraiser. When you were young did you ever say, "Gee, when I grow up I want to be a fundraiser for a nonprofit organization?" Certainly, few of us professionals did—we've often come to fundraising through a circuitous route (I started as a PR/marketing assistant for a performing arts center). This is even truer for volunteers, most of whom say, "I'll do anything other than fundraise. I'm terrible at it and hate it."

This means pushing through myriad personal challenges. Whether you don't like asking anyone for anything, or you were taught never to talk about money, or you fear rejection, there's something that creates a significant hurdle for you when it comes to asking for money.

When we add to the personal hurdles the lack of training in our profession, we have a situation where millions of wonderful, caring people bravely go out to ask, often without understanding their role or having the tools to do it well. And yet you do.

How amazing is it that you're still willing to do it? It's a testament to how deeply you care about your organizations. A testament to how driven you are to make a difference in the world. A testament to how deeply ingrained giving back is.

This book is dedicated to all of you. You're the heroes.

foreword

"Why did I have to wait this long?"

That's what I kept thinking as I read Brian Saber's new book, *Asking Styles*. I kept thinking about how effectively I could have used the book for all the years I've been coaching fundraisers on how to ask for a gift.

One size doesn't fit all. I know that. It takes different personalities and different styles to effectively ask for a gift. Brian lays this all out for us. And he tells us how to put our individual style to use.

I might have wanted to call the book *You Can Do It*. *Asking Styles* makes so much darn sense. One size does not fit all, but the book tells you what your proper size is.

This could very well become one of the most important books in our field. It is a breakthrough of a methodology that really works.

I would have called the book, *You Can Do It*—because it clearly demonstrates that no matter what personality you are or your feelings of trepidation, you will be able to secure the gift.

It's the best antidote I've read on taking the fear out of asking. It will make you successful. If you already are, it will make you more so.

For starters, I like the fact that the author tells us that as many calls as he has made, he continues to be anxious and a tiny bit stressed when making a call. I think most of us have those same heebie-jeebies. That should give us all confidence.

In the book, you read about the importance of face-to-face solicitation. If you get to make a visit, Saber says, three out of four times you get the gift.

The book is divided into four, major personality blocks. From that, Saber tells you how to determine your personality and strengths as a solicitor. There is, by the way, an Assessment that you can take that is a great guide to your solicitation-personality.

It provides a helpful guide to how to set up the appointment for the meeting. My own experience is that if you do get a visit, you're 85% on your way to getting a gift.

You learn through precisely how to make the ask because you know your style. If you are going to take someone with you, you determine who to take because of their personality traits.

Saber writes there is one personality trait that is not good at getting the gift because they never ask. I can believe that. I have had many donors tell me, "Someone from your organization came by a while back. They did a terrific job. But they never asked and never came back."

It's amazing what you don't raise when you don't ask!

And as you would expect, this book is also a superlative guide for donors and their style. Here's what I suggest.

It will take two readings. That's what I did.

I went through the first reading quite quickly. I didn't worry about any of the identifications or ideas I would be using later.

First of all, I suggest you embrace the content and the philosophy.

In the second reading, you can spend your time on descriptions. I would share with the fundraising staff your enthusiasm for the concept and bring them on board. Each should have a copy of the book. And if you're a one-person shop, review it with your CEO.

We all want to do a better job for our organization. And in the end, for all those the organization serves. This book will do it for you.

If you are at all anxious about making a call, this book will relieve you of any concerns.

I hope your desk is piled mountain high with major gift receipts and thank you letters to donors.

Jerold Panas
Author of *Asking, Power Questions* and *Born to Raise*
Jerold Panas, Linzy & Partners

introduction

I met Andrea Kihlstedt in 2002. At the time I was the deputy executive director at Hudson Guild in New York City, where we hired Andrea to be our capital campaign consultant. Together, she and I knocked it out of the park and raised $12 million for the Guild. In the process, we became a mutual admiration society.

Fast forward to 2008. After 25 years in nonprofit organizations, I had decided not to work full-time for a nonprofit again. I wanted to do something else to impact the field.

I had been a frontline fundraiser my whole career, and even though I raised tons of money and my organizations were always tickled with my results, I felt I wasn't great at my job. I always looked around and thought—well, that's not me. I can't do it that way. I don't like meeting new people (true!). I hate special events.

Andrea spent her career as a successful capital campaign consultant, trainer, and author. She was always frustrated that so many staff and volunteers left her training sessions feeling "drained, discouraged, and even more certain that they didn't have what it takes to be a successful solicitor." She saw that the field didn't do a good job of helping people use the many natural strengths they bring to the table.

Andrea had been working on the idea that there are different types of fundraisers, that there are many ways to solicit a gift, and if we want fundraisers to be authentic we need to help people learn to ask in the way that suits them best. She created the framework for the Asking Styles and was working on how to test for them. At the time she called these different types "temperaments," though, of course, they'd evolve to "styles."

Yes! This was music to my ears. Just hearing her talk about the temperaments made me feel better. I felt the calling. I knew this was the way to make a bigger impact in the field.

And in a moment of pure naiveté, we decided to start a web-based business to help people become more comfortable and effective askers. Neither of us had any idea what that meant (and absolutely no technical background whatsoever), and now we look back and laugh at how ignorant we were. It's true—ignorance is bliss!—and it enabled us to build Asking Matters, home of the Asking Styles.

In 2013, Andrea sold me her half of Asking Matters, and since then I've further developed these revolutionary Asking Styles concepts. I've watched the Asking Styles become an integral tool in the nonprofit sector. They've revolutionized people's thinking about fundraising and their role in it. They've given countless staff and board members the framework within which they could finally feel comfortable as askers.

As I've travelled the country, leading trainings and speaking at conferences, it's become clear the Asking Styles are that rare perfect antidote to a seemingly intractable issue. People love learning their Asking Style and proudly identify themselves by their Style. I've seen thousands of fundraisers become empowered right before my eyes. I've seen board members say for the first time, "OK, now I can see how I can do that."

And I've learned a TON from all of you. Your feedback has helped me hone my ability to convey important messages about asking and the Asking Styles. Your insightful questions have pushed me to think through the Asking Styles in ways I never considered.

My goal, before writing a book, was to get the material to the point where it represented a rich, detailed rubric for the nonprofit sector. And though the material will continue to bloom and there is still much to explore through the Asking Styles lens, I thought I was there. With all the experience and feedback, I finally felt ready to write the definitive guide to the Asking Styles, which I hope will strengthen our nonprofit sector and its ability to raise important dollars. I hope you'll agree.

Brian Saber
President
Asking Matters

Who Says There's Only ONE Right Way to Ask?

The breakthrough concept of the Asking Styles makes it possible for anyone to become a more effective fundraiser. Your Asking Style is based on your personality and unique set of strengths when asking for gifts.

If you've ever said to yourself "I'm not a fundraiser" or "I don't fit the stereotype," embracing your Asking Style will change your entire mind-set. Once you understand your strengths—and challenges—you'll be comfortable, confident and effective. You'll have a roadmap for dealing with donors. You'll know what to say, how to conduct meetings, and how to close gifts successfully.

one

---

why we ask in person

Let's be honest—most people don't like asking for money. In fact, most of us don't like asking for anything in fact. So, why do we not only solicit individuals for charitable gifts, but do it in person?

asking in person is unusual

These days we get solicited in lots of ways, day in and day out. Fundraising letters arrive in the mail and email solicitations hit our inbox. Our friends send us special event invitations (and we send them ours).

We get calls from those we know, such as our alma maters, and those we don't. Crowdfunding has given countless worthy projects a platform and an audience. I call this "charity shock." It's when everyone and his mother asks you for money and you feel you need a suit of armor, or at the very least a sci-fi deflector shield, to deal with the situation. There are so many worthy causes and you'd like to support them all, yet if you do so you can't give significantly to the causes you care most about.

> For all the soliciting nonprofits do, most people have never been asked face-to-face for a gift. While they might find it a bit anxiety-provoking, they'll also feel honored you took the time to meet with them.

Now ask yourself how often you've been asked in person, face-to-face, for a significant gift? I've been asking this question in my trainings for a decade, and even among board members and seasoned fundraising professionals, less than half have ever been asked. Less than half!

Now imagine how special an in-person ask is. Imagine if someone contacted you and asked to meet in person to support an organization you care about. Chances are you'd be flattered. The request would stand out from the endless, mostly generic solicitations you get. It would grab your attention. You'd think, "wow, someone wants to take the time to meet me. I'm impressed."

Asking in person is impactful because it's actually quite unusual.

asking in person is powerful

Be honest. How often do those mail solicitations go straight to the trash bin? If you know the organization or the return address you might peek inside. It's easy to ignore a mail solicitation as no one from the organization is watching you toss it. The statistics show that only 1% to 2% of all mail solicitations result in a gift, though the results for organizations you know and support will be higher.

How about the phone? Admit it. Half the time you don't pick up the phone, and the other half of the time you hang up pretty quickly, even if you know the organization. I have a personal policy of never giving over the phone. (It's partly due to my Asking Style, but I don't want to get ahead of myself here.) Research years back by Kent Dove, formerly of the Indiana University Foundation, showed that even for charities we already support and care about, only about 25% of those phone solicitations result in a gift.

Yet that same research showed that 75% of in-person asks result in a gift. Three out of four. What incredible odds! Frankly, I would make a beeline to a casino with odds like that, and I'm not a gambling man.

Why is asking in person so powerful? When we're together, a level of empathy develops that is much harder to develop by letter or by phone. The letter is a one-way communication. You get it, you read it, and that's that. You don't get to ask questions and have a back-and-forth conversation. The phone is a big step forward as we can at least hear each other's voices and start a dialog. This begins to build a relationship.

When we're in each other's company we develop an immediate bond. We find we're more interested in what the other person is saying. We want to come through for them. We want to be seen as good people who do good things. And, of course, facial expressions are key to understanding our fellow humans. In person, we develop a deeper understanding of what makes each other tick.

In an age when the smartphone is ubiquitous, and we spend more time texting, emailing, and posting than meeting in person, face time is even more precious and valuable. We crave it, and we don't take it for granted. When someone takes the time to meet with us in person, it's quite meaningful. And that's to our advantage as fundraisers.

asking in person is fruitful

Think about donor rosters in annual reports and on donor walls. Take note of the names that grace programs, rooms, and buildings. I can assure you virtually none of those gifts were requested by letter or phone call. Many charities have a story about a donor who made a whopping gift by letter or phone call, and those stories are memorable because they're so rare and surprising. Without question, the largest gifts at most organizations come from asking in person...and those gifts are larger than they would have been otherwise.

Further, the beauty of individuals is we tend to give to the same charities for many years, often in increasing amounts. Unlike institutional funders—foundations, corporations, and government sources—we are pleased that organizations can use our funding over the long haul. We get that almost everything we support will require charitable gifts going forward. And we don't tend to change our focus areas or take a year off to contemplate our corporate navel! We're very loyal.

asking in person is where the money is

According to Giving USA, more than $410 billion was given in charitable gifts in the United States in 2017. Of that amount, 70% ($287B) was in outright gifts by individuals. Another 9% ($36B) was in bequests, which of course are all by individuals. Already that accounts for 79% of all giving. Yet the number is even higher, as half of all foundation giving ($33B) was made by individual and family foundations where the decision was made by an individual, couple, or family. The only difference is the funds had been parked in some vehicle (i.e. a donor-advised fund) for tax planning, posterity, family dynamics, or some other reason. Together, almost 87% of all charitable gifts come from individuals!

2017 charitable giving

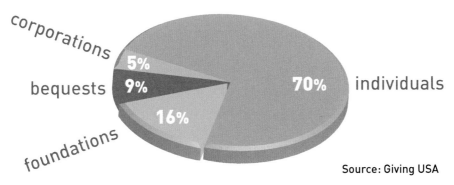

Source: Giving USA

So, with the lion's share of all charitable gifts coming from individuals, and the largest gifts coming from asking in person, the only way to fulfill your organization's vision and have the impact you want is to ask individuals for gifts face-to-face.

Does your organization spend most of its time cultivating and soliciting individuals? If you're like most organizations, you're probably knee-deep in proposals to foundations. You might be applying for government grants and looking for corporate contacts as well. Think about how much time you spend going after the slice of the pie that represents 13% of the available charitable gifts and how much time you spend on the 87%. Chances are you're not optimizing your efforts.

As for individuals, the first attempts are often around special events, direct mail, and crowdfunding, which means you're getting lots of small to mid-sized gifts. However, as with everything in life, the Pareto Principle applies: 80% of the benefit derives from 20% of the effort. This means 80% of your individual gifts will generally come from 20% of your donors. For capital campaigns, the ratio can be 90%/10% or higher. Therefore, if you are soliciting individual gifts, are you spending 80% of your time soliciting the 20% of your donors who will contribute most of the dollars?

Chances are you're not spending enough time on individual gifts and, if you are spending the time, you're not spending it on the donors who will make the biggest difference.

So, the next time someone recommends writing another proposal, sending out another letter, or creating a new event, think twice and invest that time in cultivating and soliciting individuals face-to-face.

Convinced but daunted? If the thought of soliciting individuals in person is scary, you're not alone. Most of us find it more challenging than writing proposals and dealing with foundation officers. More challenging than sending out mass appeals of one form or another. More challenging than putting on fundraising events. Let's talk about why.

two

why asking challenges us

asking is an extremely personal, I would venture to say intimate, inter-action.

Charitable giving underscores what we're passionate about, whether it's spreading the word about something we love and find enriching, such as art, or it's helping those who can't help themselves, such as children living in poverty.

Charitable giving represents our financial priorities and our money mindset. Do we think we have enough for ourselves and can share our largess with the world? Or is our list of material objects of desire so long we'll never get through it? Or do our fears of being destitute drive us to hoard our money for a rainy day?

And last but not least, charitable giving is a means of presenting ourselves to the world as we'd like to be seen. This can't be underes-

timated. Just about everyone yearns to be appreciated, admired, and liked. We're wired to want to come through for others—to be the hero, the one who solves the problem, the one who saves the day—and charitable giving helps us attain that stature among those whose opinions matter to us.

We are aware of all this, at least subconsciously, when we sit down to ask for a gift. We sense there's a lot on the line, not just for us and our organizations, but for our donors.

To the mix we add everything we, as askers, bring to the table. First off, we have our own values, our own philosophies about life and how they're reflected in our charitable giving. Being in the philanthropic field, we have strong opinions about how others should lead their charitable lives. I've certainly never met a fundraiser—professional or volunteer— who thought others generally should give less than they're currently giving. And we share with our donors the desire to be seen as good, to be seen as successful, to be liked.

We add to that a number of factors, none more insidious than fear of rejection. Over the years I've polled tens of thousands of askers, and hands down fear of rejection causes the most anxiety.

When we ask anyone for anything, we're putting ourselves on the line. We've made clear what's important to us, and it's all in the hands of whomever we've asked—our friend, our partner, our peer, our boss— to acknowledge our request, analyze its value and feasibility, and render a decision. That decision, no matter how objectively derived, is often seen as a reflection on the relationship and our personal worth. This is no less true in fundraising.

I would posit that our greatest challenge, and most important task, is remaining objective about our donor's giving. It is understanding at all times that you, as the asker, are a conduit between the organization and your donor. You are a representative of the organization, and while you have a relationship with your donor, the primary relationship is between the donor and the organization.

Easier said than done, right? We're being asked to form a close, collegial relationship with someone and then not to take things personally. Depending on how we're wired this can be incredibly difficult. I, for one, take everything personally (just ask anyone who knows me!). I'm very emotional and I lead from my heart. So, when I ask for something—anything—it comes from a deep, personal, visceral spot in my being. Keeping that at bay in my fundraising has been my greatest challenge. One can

> we sense there's a lot on the line, not just for us and our organizations, but for our donors.

only imagine how many of us "bleeding hearts" there are in fundraising since it's often that quality that draws people to the field.

Once we get past the fear of rejection, there's the fear of harming the relationship. I've always said in my next life I'll be a weather forecaster, because even if they're right only 50% of the time, they keep their jobs (is it even 50%?). For us fundraisers—particularly those of us who do it professionally—it might only take one or two significant mistakes to cause us to lose our job... or at least cause us major headaches. More than once I've seen a fundraiser shown the door over a donor relationship gone sour.

Even putting aside the fear of being reprimanded or fired, we know how important charitable gifts are to our organization and we don't want to do anything that might get in the way. We want our donors to be happy at all times, which can lead us to go too far to please them. Of course, as in any relationship, that's a mistake. We know everyone has to be responsible for their own actions, and we know, theoretically, that most everyone would like relationships to be balanced and genuine.

Yet we also have to acknowledge an often unspoken truth. Donors and askers do not have a relationship of equals. Yes, we are basically on the same side; we care about the organization and want it to have as big an impact as possible. However, the reality is that our donors can fulfill their philanthropic goals by giving to a vast array of organizations. We generally have a limited supply of donors—or prospects on the horizon—and need the support of most of them in order to fulfill our organization's goals. This is particularly true for our bread and butter—the large annual fund gifts that keep our organization in business year in and year out.

Compounding our mindset, our fears of rejection, and the imbalance in the relationship, is that virtually no one has ever been taught how to ask for gifts. Most fundraisers, and just about all volunteers, end up asking as a byproduct of some other function. Program leaders rise to become executive directors and are expected to fundraise from day one when most have never fundraised before. Board members join their first board (most are on their first board, in fact) and are expected to help fundraise. Even fundraising staff move into new positions that now require them to cultivate and solicit individuals without any training. So most of us wing it. And while we can get far on intuition, asking is both an art and a science, and being trained to ask is critical. In fact, it's training that moves us past the challenges I've identified.

Training not only gives us the basic tools we need to cultivate and solicit individuals effectively, but it helps us understand the powerful role our unique personality plays in the relationships we're building with our donors. And yes, who we are is important. While the goal is to build a strong, lifelong relationship between a donor and the organization, we who do the cultivating and asking—are critically important to the relationship. And the relationship can only be strong if you, the asker, can be authentic and embrace your unique personality.

three

authenticity is key

With all the talk about what our donors want to hear and what they want us to say, it's easy to forget that nothing is as powerful as authenticity. Authenticity is the sense that something is real, that it's based on facts and it's genuine. What you see is what you get.

You know authenticity when you see it—and you know inauthenticity when you see that. When you feel someone is being genuine, it puts you at ease. It creates a sense of trust that allows you to be genuine in turn. It allows you to be open and honest. When that's not the case, you immediately become guarded. You don't feel comfortable sharing anything personal because you worry about how that information will be perceived. You'll do your best to steer clear of this inauthentic person.

Yet, even understanding how important authenticity is, for some reason you've been taught to believe you have to be someone or something specific when you serve as a fundraiser. Maybe you think you need to show your donor that you know it all and can answer every question. Or you have to be charming and witty. Or you should be very assertive in negotiating with the donor, which might end up feeling pushy to both of you. You can start to feel inauthentic and awkward trying to be something you're not.

Through the Asking Styles we'll learn there's no one right way to ask for a gift and that means there's no one right way to be. We all need to be ourselves. When we're ourselves we're authentic.

For years I thought I wasn't a very good fundraiser because there were parts of fundraising I disliked, in particular large gatherings and special events. I always felt out of place and could often be found out in the hallway if that were at all possible. I was much more interested in being with people in small groups or, even better, one on one. Of course, I came to realize this was a great strength in major gift fundraising.

I also used to be frustrated because I didn't focus on the quantitative accomplishments of organizations I represented and thought that was interfering with my being a strong fundraiser. I am an intuitive and have a gut feeling as to whether I believe in an organization's work and I've always presented my case to donors in a very personal, mission-driven way. It always felt inauthentic to me to try and muster up enthusiasm for facts and figures when what I really wanted to do was tell a participant story or a personal story about my journey.

You also convey a number of very important characteristics, including sincerity, honesty, reliability, and trustworthiness. People sense you mean what you say. Because you seem to be sincere and honest, they feel they can rely on you to do the right thing by them. They feel they can trust you to be honest about the organization's work and how their gifts will be used. When you're authentic you garner respect from your donor.

When you are your authentic self you'll have the added benefit of feeling confident in what you're saying. Think of an instance when you felt you had to be less than forthcoming, or tell a white lie, or in some way not be 100% honest and open. It takes a lot of effort as you've got to use your wits to navigate the situation. You've got to work hard to "sell" that information...or to withhold it. When you're authentic everything comes easier. That's not to say delivering honest messages can't sometimes be difficult. We're faced with situations like that all the time, but when we do share honest messages, it's freeing. As in any relationship, your donors can sense all this.

> **TIP:**
>
> ---
>
> Be your great, authentic self. You'll feel comfortable in your own skin and your donor will feel—and appreciate—that authenticity.

Your donors can also sense your authenticity the first time they meet you. The science of first impressions has been studied extensively and the evidence is clear. When we meet someone, we only have a few seconds—seven seconds in fact—to make a first impression. Once we've made a first impression, it takes a long time, if ever, to change it.

There are many ways to make a good first impression. You can be courteous and attentive. You can be confident. You can be positive. We've often heard a smile or a solid handshake makes an impact. In building a donor relationship, what could be more important than your authenticity? What could be more important than your donor thinking from the get-go that you're genuine, sincere, and trustworthy. Would you be motivated to build any philanthropic relationship that doesn't have authenticity at its core? When you're not sure you can trust the organization because it's represented by someone you think isn't authentic, it's over before it's begun.

So how does our authenticity come through? How do we demonstrate it? Though authenticity has one meaning, it has many manifestations. We each show it in different ways.

Some of us share personal stories. This has always been a strong point for me. I'm a sharer. Some have accused me of TMI. I think sharing personal stories helps our donors see and know us as human beings, since by nature they see us as representatives of the organization whose job it is to solicit their gift. As with anything else, the more we get to know people the harder it is to stereotype them.

T.M.I. stands for "too much information." In my private life I call myself The King of T.M.I. I've always found it easier to share just about everything than to constantly monitor and edit myself. I put a lot of information in the hands of others with the trust that most people are good and will be considerate, non-judgmental, and trustworthy. That's generally worked out!

> The sharing of our personal stories shows donors we're authentic and it builds trust.

Sharing our stories encourages donors to share theirs. When they do, we learn more about them and what we have in common, which further benefits the relationship we're building.

Some of us show authenticity by expressing our feelings. We share what we're thinking, how the world around us is impacting us, and what our hopes and fears might be. Most importantly, we share how we feel about our organization and why it's so important to us to raise funds for it. Sharing our feelings shows vulnerability, and vulnerability feels authentic. And, as with stories, it encourages our donors to share their feelings and be vulnerable with us.

Some of us are spontaneous. We blurt things out. We take a chance and ask an out-of-the-blue question or take the conversation in a slightly unexpected direction. For those who demonstrate their authenticity through spontaneity, it helps counter the risk that the donor will sense everything is scripted and that we basically treat every meeting the same way.

Some of us readily admit what we don't know. There's a sense in fundraising that you have to know everything and have an answer for every question a donor might ask. As we'll discuss later I don't think this is true at all. I'm OK saying "I actually don't know that answer, but I'll find it out and get back to you quickly." Not only am I OK saying it, but in showing I don't have all the answers I demonstrate my authenticity.

And some of us use humor, which can show another side of ourselves...including our willingness to fall flat! Remember, awkward is fine—and can even be charming—especially for volunteers and young or less-experienced askers. In fact, as a professional, I sometimes worry I can be perceived as slick in having the perfect answer for everything and always being able to phrase things effortlessly. So, in sharing my stories and feelings, acknowledging what I don't know, and throwing out jokes that sometimes don't land, I get an awkward moment here and there, but my authenticity shines through.

I hope you can see that authenticity is critically important to fundraising. Being who you truly are will lead to stronger donor relationships and greater giving. So, how do you maintain your authenticity as an asker? Enter the Asking Styles.

four

---

enter the asking styles

---

i will never forget the inimitable audition scene from the 1982 film "Tootsie," where the Dustin Hoffman character, an actor who's desperate for a part, tries negotiating with the director:

"I can be taller."

"No. We're looking for somebody shorter."

"Look. I don't have to be this tall. See, I'm wearing lifts. I can be shorter."

"I know, but we're looking for somebody different."

"I can be different."

"We're looking for somebody else."

The biggest mistake fundraisers can make is thinking we need to be something we're not; thinking there's some ideal fundraiser who has it all, and if we can just be like that person we'd be really successful. Here's the kicker. The only personality type that is not good at getting the gift...is the one that never asks!

the ideal

We all have that ideal image in our mind. Someone comfortable at all times, who clearly and confidently asks for a gift and then negotiates successfully to a "yes" regardless of the first response. Someone who always asks the right questions, gets the donor to share important information, and answers any question that comes his way. He's got all the facts and figures on instant recall and can tell moving stories about the organization's work and its participants. And if he gets rejected, it's no big deal—he's on to the next prospect. Oh, and he loves meeting new people and seems to turn every Joe Schmo around the corner into a major donor overnight.

> **TIP:**
>
> There's no such thing as a perfect fundraiser. No one has it all. We all play to our strengths.

If you know anyone like that, please introduce me!

the stereotype

Our donors—and the general public—have an even more insidious picture of a fundraiser. They see a hardcore salesman always out to close the deal. Someone like the "Tootsie" character who will do just about anything to get a "yes." First of all, though some salespeople feel like this (for me it's car salespeople), in fact, many of the best salespeople are not like this at all. For them it's about building a relationship, just as it is for fundraisers.

There's no ideal and the stereotypes generally have little to do with who we are. Thinking we're supposed to be something we're not—and may not want to be—will only hold us back from being the best we can be.

the asking styles

The Asking Styles directly address the myth of the ideal and stereotypical fundraiser. They're based on the concept that authenticity is key to building a relationship, and building a relationship is key to fundraising. This means fundraisers must be true to themselves in order to be comfortable, confident, and effective fundraisers.

So, what are the key characteristics of an asker? I believe two predominate: how we interact and how we think. Let's explore them both.

how we interact

How we interact—or behave—with others is at the root of all relationships. Some of us are naturally garrulous while others are quiet and more introspective. Some of us get excited when meeting new people, while others find it anxiety-provoking. Some of us do well in big groups and others shine in one-on-one situations.

Think of the last party or event you attended. Maybe it was one of your organization's special events. How did you feel? Were you excited to attend, or did you go because you had to? How did you behave at the time? Did you enthusiastically jump into and out of conversations, or did you find yourself huddled in the corner with one person? And afterward, did you think, "wow, I'm revved up... where's the next event?" Perhaps you're an extrovert. Or did you think, "get me home... I need to recharge." Perhaps you're an introvert.

People mistakenly think introverts don't like to socialize. This isn't the case. Introverts find great reward in their relationships with others, yet those interactions can often use their energy, leaving them yearning to refuel with some quiet alone time. This use of energy derives from the fact that introverts think to talk. They like to stop and think about what they're going to say before actually saying it. They need that bit of time to process information and formulate their thoughts. That might be a second or two, but it contrasts significantly with the extrovert, who talks to think.

Think back to that function you attended. Picture everyone milling about, coming in and out of conversations, and think of how rapid fire the dialog was. Did you feel you were in the mix, able to jump in and be heard? Or did it seem that every time you were about to say something—after pausing to think of what to say—someone else jumped in and you practically had to cut someone off to get a word in edgewise? If you were comfortably in the mix, you're probably an extrovert. If you were constantly frustrated, or found yourself spurting out comments without enough thought, you're probably an introvert.

how do you interact with people?

extrovert =	derive energy from others	talk to think
introvert =	derive energy from oneself	think to talk

People always assume I'm an extrovert because I've mastered the art of conversation. They see me as confident and articulate and willing to engage those around me. What they don't understand is how much practice that's taken over my lifetime, and how much energy I expend in these interactions. Those who know me best know I turn down almost every party invite... and every opportunity to meet new people. It just feels like so much work! We'll talk about how this has impacted my fundraising a bit later.

How we interact—where we are on the spectrum of extroversion/introversion—is the vertical axis of the Asking Styles.

A word on "the spectrum." Try not to think in absolutes here. Many people believe they're not extroverts because they don't resemble some loud, overbearing person who monopolizes conversations and always hogs the attention (think Michael Scott from "The Office") Or they believe they're not introverts because they assume introverts are hermits (think Shrek).

While some people certainly resemble those caricatures, most of us are somewhere safely in between. That gives us the tools to make our way in the world, interact positively with a wide range of

> TIP:
>
> ---
>
> Introverted doesn't mean anti-social, socially awkward or shy. Anyone— whether introvert or extrovert—can have those characteristics.

people, and be successful in our work. We also use different parts of our personality at different times depending on the situation and the personalities of those around us. That doesn't mean we're trying to be anything we're not. We're simply reading the situation and acting appropriately in it.

how you interact impacts how you fundraise

We know introverts aren't going to love their organizations' special events. These will be rather trying moments that we introverts tolerate because they come with the territory. As the extroverts jump into the fray (and we're so grateful to you for doing this!), we're likely to be found in a corner or along a wall. If we're lucky. we'll wrangle one poor sucker to talk to us the entire time. I can't tell you how often I've only semi-jokingly offered my fellow staff a huge donation to our cause if I could skip a function.

Putting special events aside, what does all this mean for cultivating and soliciting individuals face-to-face?

Extroverts, those who talk to think, tend to talk more readily and more often, while introverts, who think to talk, tend to talk more cautiously and less often. In a conversation you're either talking or listening, so extroverts talk more and introverts listen more.

Coming back to the spectrum, if you're in the middle of the spectrum the talking and listening might be very balanced for you. But what about the rest of us?

Extroverts open conversations easily—by phone and in person. Extroverts are much more comfortable picking up the phone to talk to a donor. They're more likely to use the phone to set up meetings (more on that later) and are adept at keeping the conversation on track and thinking quickly on their feet when the conversation goes off the rails. Introverts are more likely to send an email as the pace of an email conversation gives us the time to think before talking. Email has been my best friend for almost 30 years, and I credit my longevity and success to being able to use email rather than the phone. We'll talk more about this in Chapter 8.

In the solicitation meeting itself, extroverts excel at opening the conversation as everyone is settling into the meeting. Introverts need a few minutes to get into the rhythm and this could mean some awkward gaps in the opening conversation.

Extroverts always have to remember not to dominate the conversation—especially if they're meeting with introverts. Their goal is to learn about donors by asking lots of questions, and they can't do that if they're spending the time talking. Since introverts think to talk, they naturally take the time to pause before speaking, which allows space for others to speak. They also enjoy listening and observing.

how we think

As I started to write this book I looked back on my three longest, most successful stints and realized they all had one thing in common—bosses who just let me go out and do what I do best. Ron Manderschied (Northwestern Settlement House), Nancy Winship (Brandeis University), and Janice McGuire (Hudson Guild) saw that I had the chops and the motivation to cultivate and solicit individual donors, and they didn't try to guide me or rein me in.

They understood who I was and knew instinctively I wouldn't do well providing them tons of metrics or constant reporting back. They trusted me to always do the right thing by donors while never compromising the institution. They knew I was very responsible and motivated to come through. Their intuition told them they could trust me.

Intuitive people have a gut feeling. Something in their head or heart says, "this is possible" or "this feels right." Based on that gut feeling they act. They don't run the numbers or conduct some deep analysis. They leap ahead. They act. And then they find out if their gut was right.

Let's use as an example online dating, where a good friend and I take very different approaches. I scroll through the Match.com profiles, see a picture or two and read a brief statement, and have a gut reaction about the potential. Of course, as an introvert I'm less likely to reach out, but once a guy reaches out to me I'm willing to meet based on a few emails or a quick phone call. Not my friend. She needs tons of information and a fair amount of interaction before that first date.

> **TIP:**
>
> ---
>
> **Everything in this book is applicable to your relationships with institutional funders. At the end of the day, people give to people. Forming authentic relationships with funders is key to most institutional gifts.**

The second date is even more revealing. If I have a good first date I'm happy (motivated) to have the second date the next day. My gut has told me this could be something, so why not pursue it? No matter how much my friend likes her date, she won't go on the second one for some time. She needs to take it slowly and methodically. She needs to analyze the situation.

How we think—where on the spectrum of analytic/intuitive we are—is the horizontal axis of the Asking Styles.

how you think impacts how you fundraise

Whether you're analytic or intuitive impacts why you care about your organization—perhaps what motivated you to join it in the first place—and how you talk about it.

Analytics are driven by the data. Whether it's a goal, a strategic plan, or just the facts and figures, this concrete and quantifiable information excites you and convinces you an impact can be made. In fact, without this information the organization's vision is difficult to embrace. It will seem like pie in the sky and you're not likely to enthusiastically support it.

how do you take in information?

	inductive		deductive
analytic =	fact-oriented	intuitive=	idea-oriented
	data to idea		idea to data

Intuitives are driven by an idea. You sense something—get something in your head or heart—and it drives you. You have faith in your gut and move ahead based on that. Perhaps you hear a story of a program participant whose life has been transformed, or you meet a staff person and are inspired by their work.

When we put the two axes together, we get the four Asking Styles:

Rainmaker: Analytic Extrovert
Go-Getter: Intuitive Extrovert
Kindred Spirit: Intuitive Introvert
Mission Controller: Analytic Introvert

Do you have a gut feeling as to which Asking Style you are? Per-haps you're more likely to have a gut feeling—or believe strongly in that gut feeling—if you're an intuitive. If you're an analytic you might still need more information before making a decision. And if you're think-ing more than one Asking Style could be you, this could very well be the case. As you'll learn in the next chapter, most of us have "primary" and "secondary" Asking Styles.

five

---

the four asking styles

Let's walk through each Asking Style now. As you read the descriptions, think not only of yourself, but also your whole team. Who comes to mind? Later in the book we'll talk about how the various Styles interact and what this might mean for your fundraising and your teamwork.

Rainmakers

Analytic Extroverts: What's the Goal?

fact based
goal oriented
strategic
competitive
driven

Rainmakers are the Analytic Extroverts. When people think of a fundraiser they think of you. They think of someone who confidently and objectively heads out the door to conquer the world and is strategically—and competitively—driven to achieve a goal.

It's true that when a Rainmaker is trying to figure out why something should matter, the goal is key. And you keep driving toward that goal, objectively. But it doesn't mean you close gifts at any cost; your every move is strategic. You are competitive and like to come out on top, and you get there by keeping your eye on the prize.

You like to be well-informed and will take the time to sift through detailed information, in particular strategic plans. The more concrete information you have the more compelling the case for support you can make.

Analytics are objective, following the facts. As someone who is extroverted and objective you can be successful with a wide range of donors. You don't take things personally, and everything is evaluated through the prism of whether someone is or might be an important donor. Not taking things personally allows you to put rejection in its place. You clearly understand it's no reflection on you but rather on where the donor is in their relationship with the organization and with their philanthropy. Further, you know their perspective might change over time and you might even relish having to work a bit harder to get a gift. You're also willing to reach out to long shots and new prospects as you enjoy the challenge of turning them into donors.

Fun anecdote: I've worked with the United States Olympic Committee over the years. A few years back I led a webinar for their fundraisers from across the country. When I polled them on their Asking Style, more than 90% identified as Rainmakers. At first, I was taken aback, until I realized many of them are current or former competitive athletes—of course they're goal-oriented and driven!

Does Rainmaker sound like you?

Go-Getters

Intuitive Extroverts: What's the Opportunity?

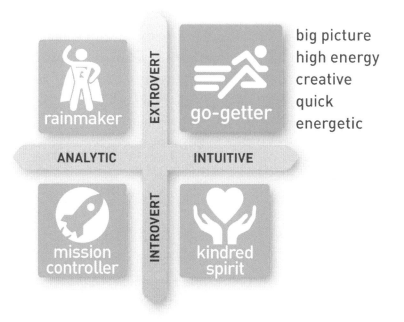

big picture
high energy
creative
quick
energetic

In full disclosure, I love Go-Getters... until you guys drive me crazy!

Go-Getters have an infectious high-energy personality. You're passionate about the world and those around you, and you make friends quickly and easily. When I think of a Go-Getter I think of the life of the party – someone who energizes a room, naturally links people together, and comfortably goes from conversation to conversation. Oh, and Go-Getters never arrive at a party until it's going strong! Are you nodding your head?

Go-Getters have a vision that comes from your gut, and you pursue that vision confidently. While some of your ideas might fall flat, your willingness to take a chance and put yourself out there means lots of great things happen. And because you put it out there confidently, people are eager to follow along.

Your natural inquisitiveness serves you well. You love meeting with old and new donors alike and learning about them. In fact, you're likely to befriend them over time.

And you're big fans of interactive process. You love talking through ideas aloud and enjoy the back-and-forth debate. It took my co-founder Andrea (Go-Getter) and me (Kindred Spirit) a few years to figure out how to work together. We finally agreed meetings should be no longer than about 45 minutes. Though she could be in the moment for hours, we found that my eyes glazed over after about 45 minutes and I could no longer hear anything she was saying.

Over the past year I've worked closely with Judi Smith, Director of Planned Giving at the Arizona Community Foundation. Judi is a proud Go-Getter. Every time she asks me to send her information again because she can't find it, she says "don't you wish I had a little Mission Controller in me?" I tell her I'd never sacrifice any of her big-picture thinking and infectious enthusiasm, and she can count on my Secondary Asking Style of Mission Controller (more on that soon) to keep us, and our work together, on track.

Do you think you're a Go-Getter?

Kindred Spirits

Intuitive Introverts: What Moves My Heart?

feelings oriented
attentive
caring
thoughtful
selfless

I'm a classic Kindred Spirit—an Intuitive Introvert. We're feelings oriented and wear our hearts on our sleeves. Our decisions emanate from what we're feeling deep down. We use our gut just like Go-Getters do, but our gut comes from a deeper, more personal spot.

We take everything personally. In fact, even after 30+ years in the business I still have to remind myself that I'm only the messenger. Whatever the donor's response, it's about where the donor is at personally, charitably, and in her relationship with the organization. I have to tell myself that often.

Being very sensitive ourselves, we tend to project that onto others and assume they're sensitive as well, and so we treat them with much attention and care. We're always asking people what we can do for them. We want them to feel good, to feel they've been heard and seen.

We try hard to avoid awkward moments. Getting to know our donors involves asking lots of questions, some of which can be quite personal. Our fear of creating an awkward moment by asking too personal a question—or simply a question our donor doesn't want to answer—will feel like conflict and can keep us from asking that question.

When we do make a mistake or unintentionally hurt someone, we feel it deeply. It gets in our bones and we have a hard time forgiving ourselves. That makes us extra cautious—perhaps too cautious—in dealing with donors.

Though our decisions are intuitive like those of Go-Getters, we don't make them as quickly. We appreciate the opportunity to take some time and consider thoughts away from the pressure of an immediate response. As Andrea and I figured out our work relationship, we realized that I couldn't always respond to her ideas in the moment and that she shouldn't take my silence as rejection of them, but rather as my need to step back and think through them on my own.

Could you be a Kindred Spirit?

Mission Controllers

Analytic Introverts: What's the Plan?

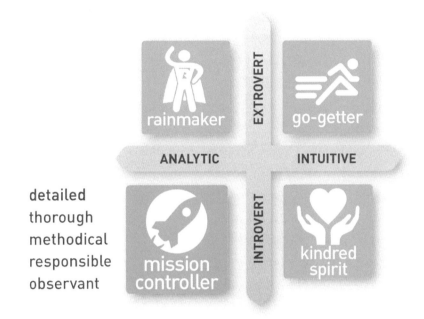

Where would we be without Mission Controllers—the Analytic Introverts? Mission Controllers keep everything moving along when the rest of us might veer off course. You always get the job done.

Mission Controllers are detailed and thorough. You're great researchers, motivated to dig in and dig deep. And no matter how much research you do, you're likely to think there's more to be done. You'll leave no stone unturned.

You make decisions thoughtfully after reviewing all the available information. You're wired to ask for information in advance of meetings rather than being presented with it in the moment. If someone brings material to a meeting, that can throw you as you know you won't be able to review it in detail.

If the information before you is incomplete or unclear, you'll methodically ask a series of questions until you're satisfied. They're never meant to challenge, but to clarify. And in doing so you play a critical role in helping others clarify their own thoughts.

Everything for the Mission Controller stems from a detailed plan and the systems to implement it because you don't see the value of vision if there's no plan to support it. Without a plan and systems, individual actions have no meaning or context. Given your passion for planning, you're likely to be assigned that role, as others know they can count on you. Even if you're not assigned by others, you're likely to nominate yourself to ensure the work gets done.

Mission Controllers are great listeners—often the best listeners of everyone in the room. You're comfortable being quiet among others and enjoy the role of observer. When you do chime in, it will be with a well- thought-out remark. But people will need to make space for you and invite your participation, as you're not likely to jump into the fray.

Do you think you're a Mission Controller?

secondary asking styles

Having heard the four descriptions, which Asking Style sounds like you? Is there a clear winner? If not, don't worry. The Secondary Asking Styles will help you figure that out.

Are you thinking you're a little bit of this and a little bit of that? For most of us even though one Asking Style stands out, we see a fair amount of another Style in us as well. Few of us fit neatly and completely in one quadrant or another. Those who do I call the "uber-Rainmakers," "uber-Go-Getters," etc. The "ubers" are in the farthest corners of the grid, where both characteristics are equally, and significantly, dominant.

For most of us, one characteristic is more dominant than the other. Either our extroversion, introversion, analytic thinking, or intuitive thinking dominates. To reflect this, we also identify a Secondary Asking Style.

my primary/secondary asking styles

Although my Primary Asking Style is Kindred Spirit, my Secondary Asking Style is Mission Controller, which means how I interact (my introversion) is more dominant than how I think. Though I definitely think from the heart and make decisions based on my gut, I actually have facility in numbers, calculations, facts and figures. In fact, I've always loved math. I also have an interest in having things organized. Though I never seem to get to the point where I feel I'm organized enough, I have come to realize that relative to most people I'm rather organized!

If your dominant trait is extroversion, you will find it interesting meeting new prospects and you'll find you can comfortably engage a wide range of people in a broad set of situations. You'll easily get conversations going and move them along, and these interactions will give you energy. However, you do have a tendency to talk too much, which is the curse of death in fundraising as our goal is to listen and learn (more on that later), so your challenge will be keeping that in check and ensuring your prospects do the talking.

Not true for those whose dominant trait is introversion. To the contrary, you will excel at listening and giving prospects the room to speak. Since your natural tendency is to pause to think before talking, you create natural moments of quiet your prospects can fill. And because your preference is not to be the focal point of a conversation or situation, you happily give that spotlight to others. Your challenges will be your limited desire to meet new people and the amount of energy those meetings take. You'll need to refuel often.

> For most of us, one characteristic is more dominant than the other.

The analytic/intuitive dichotomy is also interesting. Analytics will excel at internalizing the facts, figures, outcomes, and plans of the organization, and at sharing those in a compelling way with prospects. The intuitives will excel at creating and sharing inspiring personal stories—of your own journey and those of participants. Analytics will be challenged to find and share those stories, while the intuitives will find themselves working hard to embrace the organization's objective, factual information. We'll talk more about this when we cover developing your case for support in Chapter 7.

Which do you think is your dominant trait?

primary   secondary

Extroversion:

      Rainmaker   Go-Getter

      Go-Getter   Rainmaker

Introversion:

      Mission Controller   Kindred Spirit

      Kindred Spirit   Mission Controller

Analytic thinking:

      Rainmaker   Mission Controller

      Mission Controller   Rainmaker

Intuitive thinking:

      Go-Getter   Kindred Spirit

      Kindred Spirit   Go-Getter

are you ready to find out for sure?

It's time to take the Asking Style Assessment, a free 30 question, true/false assessment you can take online right now. The assessment only takes three minutes to complete. Be sure not to overthink the questions (that means you, Mission Controllers!)—answer them based on your first thought. You will get a result immediately on screen, with a copy emailed to you. The result will include your Primary and Secondary Asking Styles and a description of your core strengths.

take the assessment

www.askingmatters.com/find-your-style

Once you've taken the Assessment, come back to continue reading the book. We'll spend the next five chapters talking about how to use your Asking Style throughout the asking process.

your results

So, what did you think? Did your Asking Styles Assessment results match your original thoughts? Or were the results different? If they were different, did reading the description change your mind?

If you're feeling "I'm not buying the results... I don't think they capture who I am" it may very well mean your true self is close to the origin of the axes:

If you're close to the origin, you've got relatively equal amounts of the various qualities that imbue each Style. This can be a great asset, as it may mean you're more adaptable to the various situations and personalities you'll encounter in your fundraising.

So don't worry if you're still unsure. Either choose the Style that feels a bit more like you than the others, or don't choose one and take away from each chapter what resonates for you. And you might find you've got a stronger sense after finishing the book.

MORE THAN 30,000 people have taken the Assessment. Here are some reactions from the field:

Knowing my Asking Style makes me a better storyteller about my cause. I'm more confident, passionate and authentic. Donors respond to that!

—Lauren Phipps, Director of Development,
Ochsner Baptist at Ochsner Health System, New Orleans

The profile nailed me. Furthermore, it did it in a flattering way, highlighting my strengths instead of telling me "things I should work on."

—Paul Jolly, Lead Consultant,
Jump Start Growth, Inc., Washington, DC

Love it! Totally fits!

—Keiren Havens, Chief Strategy Officer
Health Care for the Homeless, Baltimore, MD

All I can say is "duh." You pegged me perfectly. I think you thought "mmm, Go-Getter with Kindred Spirit rising? What is Mary Hedahl like?" Then filled in the blanks. The profile was spot on. I love it.

—Mary Hedahl, Former Director of Development
New York ACLU

It has revolutionized my fundraising to know that I can work with my own personality style (Kindred Spirit/Mission Controller) to be successful.

— Kylie Pierce, Development Director,
Rome Capitol Theatre, Rome, NY

Uncannily accurate.

— Jerry Cincola, Editor, Contributions Magazine

six

how each asking style selects prospects

five steps of the ask

At Asking Matters we developed the Five Steps of the Ask to frame the asking process start to finish. It all begins with selecting the right prospects; if you're soliciting the wrong people you won't get very far. Once you've identified whom to solicit, you need to prepare for the solicitation. I always say you can't reach out to set up the meeting without having done your preparation, because communicating with someone about finding a time to meet could well become the solicitation itself.

Setting up the meeting is a step unto itself because it's such a critical moment in the process. If you set it up correctly you're almost guaranteed a gift. The fourth step is the actual solicitation meeting, after which you need to follow through. Follow through is not just the steps you take immediately afterward to encourage, close, and acknowledge a gift, but what you do going forward to keep your donor engaged.

selecting prospects

Good prospects for individual face-to-face cultivation and solicitation share a number of characteristics. They have the ability to make a gift at whatever threshold you've set (see sidebar). They have some belief in your organization or the kind of work you do. And they either are in contact with you, or someone in your circle of influence can make contact. These prospects include current donors, volunteers, program participants, friends of board members, and others.

However, just because someone is a good prospect doesn't mean that prospect is your best match. Of course, in some cases you're the only person available and you have to cultivate and solicit a wide range of people regardless of the fit with your personality. Or you're a major gift officer with a set portfolio. If so, Chapter 11, on how donors and askers interact based on the Asking Styles, will be particularly important to you.

If you do have the choice of picking from a larger pool of prospects, the Asking Styles can create a great roadmap for matching askers and donors. This is particularly important for board members. Board members will rarely be as adept at fundraising as professionals, which makes the fit between them and their prospects that much more important.

When figuring out who to cultivate and solicit, set a "threshold" for giving. The "threshold" is the minimum potential gift a donor would have to make in order to be worthy of the time/effort/money it takes to cultivate and solicit the donor in person. What level is that for your organization—$1,000? $5,000? $25,000? Whatever that level is, once you set it try your best to make very few exceptions. There might be someone with a special relationship (board member?) who can't meet the threshold, or an important member of the community with limited capacity, but be as diligent as possible to ensure you're spending your time on your best donors.

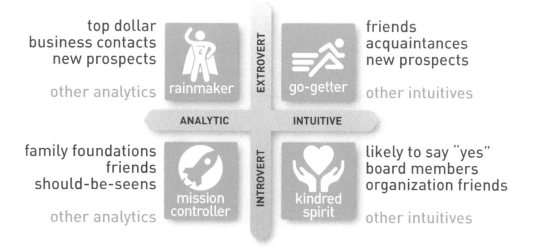

rainmakers

Rainmakers are ideally suited to pursue the organization's top prospects. You're goal-oriented, and your competitive nature fuels your desire to close big gifts. The bigger the gift the more motivated you are, and you have no interest in closing smaller gifts.

If you're a volunteer who's a Rainmaker, you're excellent at mining your Rolodex (millennials might have to Google this word) for work purposes and strategic in how you do so. This transfers to your personal life, where you're willing to use your business contacts strategically for the organizations you love. It helps that you approach everything objectively and can live with whatever response you get.

Rainmakers are great matches for those no one has met with before, whether new prospects or donors no one has contacted previously. As extroverts, you enjoy meeting new people, and the challenge of turning a new prospect into a donor—or taking a modest donor and turning her into a major donor—excites you.

go-getters

Go-Getters are also solid matches for new prospects. Go-Getters love meeting new people and you make friends easily. You have great curiosity about others and a natural inquisitiveness that makes conversing easy. You may not be as strategic as Rainmakers when meeting new people, but you're equally willing and able.

You will also mine your connections because you love connecting the various strands of your lives. For you it's "all for one and one for all." Though you're willing to connect business contacts, you most excel at opening the door to your friends and acquaintances.

kindred spirits

Don't ask Kindred Spirits to solicit those they know well. It took me 25 years to stop soliciting my friends and family, to realize I would always take their lack of support personally and that it would impact our relationship. It's always going to be personal for me, and while I can put that in perspective when soliciting my organization's prospects, I can't when I bring my own network to the table.

If you're just starting out, don't pursue the big fish or the challenging prospects. Start with those likely to say yes, such as current donors, board members, and other friends of the organization, where the question isn't so much whether someone will contribute but how much someone will contribute. It's critically important you get your sea legs—get some wins under your belt—to build your confidence and put any future rejection in perspective.

mission controllers

Mission Controllers are a great match for family foundations. Family foundations are similar to individuals in that they represent an individual or family's money, but what works in your favor here is that they are a bit more formal, structured, and systematic, and that fits with your organized and methodical approach. Usually the foundation will have guidelines and deadlines, and there might a proposal on the table that frames the meeting. This brings structure and formality to the meetings themselves and you work well in this environment.

When it comes to your personal circle, you're willing to cultivate and solicit your friends and family. You see the task at hand in an objective and methodical way. It makes sense to systematically approach your network and see what happens.

And I always say assign a Mission Controller "should be seens"— donors who might only give if they're seen. Can you think of someone who had a bad experience with your organization with whom you sense you need to smooth things out? Perhaps the person had a bad seat at your gala, wasn't thanked appropriately for something, or is a little concerned about where the program is headed. You might not get continued gifts without hearing this donor out and calming the waters. That's a "should-be-seen."

fellow analytics and intuitives

The analytic/intuitive dichotomy is an interesting filter for choosing prospects. If you and your prospect are both analytic or both intuitive, you speak a similar language and enjoy a similar process.

Speaking the same language makes it easier to tell your story—your case for support—which we'll discuss in the next chapter, and easier to answer questions as they arise. If you and your prospect are analytics, you'll naturally share information your prospect finds most resonant. If you're both intuitives, your personal stories will resonate.

If you share a process mindset, your styles of setting up meetings, having discussions, and following through are likely to be similar. For instance, as a Mission Controller you'll want to send your prospect lots of information in advance of meeting. A Mission Controller or Rainmaker prospect will appreciate all that material. A Go-Getter or Kindred Spirit prospect could be overwhelmed with it, which means either she's a bit frustrated to receive all that material or you're a bit frustrated that you can't send it.

seven

---

how each style prepares the ask

Preparing the ask is the biggest and most important step—yes, more important than the actual ask. The better prepared you are, the more successful you will be. OK, now as I wrote that I thought to myself, "Brian, you have just given Mission Controllers license to prepare and prepare and prepare some more, and still not head out the door because they're still preparing!" And at the same time, I've probably just lost some of the Go-Getters who are comfortable and happy winging it—no research, no strategizing, no practice... just out the door you go! Our goal is a happy medium, understanding we'll all prepare differently and at different intensities.

conducting prospect research and reviewing organization materials

Before reaching out to set up meetings, you need to learn about your donors. If you try to set up a meeting and don't at least know the basics about your donor, you'll make a terrible impression. Your organization might have a file on your donor already, or you might have to learn more by doing research.

Rainmakers and Mission Controllers will, by your analytic nature, want to gather as much information as possible before reaching out. You'll want to be super prepared, especially you Mission Controllers. You'll both want to conduct in-depth wealth screening, gathering of biographical information, and gleaning of overall philanthropic interests and patterns of giving. And Mission Controllers, no matter how much information you gather you will still think you need more.

Not so true for Go-Getters and Kindred Spirits (especially if your Secondary Asking Style is also one of the two). If someone were to put all that information in front of you, chances are you wouldn't read it anyway. You'll be much better served with summary information and a one-page bio, which you'll actually review.

Based on your Asking Style, you'll seek out different types of information. The analytics will focus on gift history, wealth indicators, and other factual information, while intuitives will dig deeper into biographical information and understanding the donors' personal stories and connections to your organization.

I'm sure the analytics are saying, "but wait, why shouldn't we know as much as possible?" Yes, in an ideal world the more you know the better. However, we can only absorb what we can absorb, and we don't want an ideal to stand in the way of our getting out the door. Further, keep in mind that much of the best—and most accurate—information comes from the meeting itself, and from what you learn cumulatively over the years as you continue the dialog.

The same concepts hold for gathering information about your organization. If you're a staff member you probably already know enough, though you might want to refresh your memory. If you're new to the staff or a volunteer, getting up to speed will be more important.

The analytics will devour facts and figures, with Rainmakers focusing on strategic documents and outcomes (goals) measurements while Mission Controllers will read through annual plans and try to learn how programs are delivered.

Intuitives will be looking for program and participant stories, with Go-Getters reaching out to program staff to learn what's new, while Kindred Spirits will want to experience a program directly and, if possible, meet with participants to hear directly from them. Kindred Spirits will also reflect on their own personal journeys as they relate to the organization's mission.

your case for support

Often when people hear "case for support," they conjure up one of those lengthy documents or videos developed for a capital campaign: a map to the future which talks about everything the organization wants to accomplish down the road and everything it will take—new staff, new structures, more endowed funds, etc.

When we talk about cultivating and soliciting donors face-to-face, the case for support is not a document or any written or physical thing. It's your story. It's a story of why the organization is meaningful to you. It's a story of why you care.

It must be a story told passionately and authentically, and that will only be the case if it's a story based on what moves you. It can't be the organization's "elevator pitch," something everyone is expected to recite to everyone they meet. If it is, you definitely won't sound passionate unless you've got great acting chops, and if you do try to sell words that aren't yours, you won't sound authentic. If you're not authentic your donors will sense that and it will be difficult to build the relationship.

Over the years I've been asked countless times, "don't I need to tell the donor what the donor wants to hear?" Yes, but what a donor wants to hear is your enthusiasm, passion, and authenticity. If your presentation doesn't touch on everything donors are curious about, they'll ask you questions. And, frankly, how often do you really know in advance what your donors want to hear? The ideal is to know your donors well before soliciting them, but the reality is that we get much less face time than we'd like. Often, in the solicitation meetings themselves, we're learning a lot about what makes donors tick.

Best practice is for your case for support to focus on vision and impact. While it's often easier to talk about the organization's needs, gifts in support of vision are bigger. When your donors are asked to support a need of your organization—such as more space for programming—they'll contribute something. We're a caring society and people respond when asked to help. But gifts of need are small. Gifts of need are bandages on a wound. If you talk about the vision your organization has for what it can accomplish with more space, your donors can see themselves partnering with you to fulfill that vision. Their gifts feel like investments in a better future. And gifts that feel like investments will be larger.

How about impact? Do you find yourself reciting a litany of deadening facts, such as 500 meals a day for seniors, four state-of-the-art science labs, a new bus with interactive exhibits, etc.? These are the features of your organization. As proud as you are of those 500 meals, what's more impressive is the impact you have on seniors because of those meals. Ask yourself what the benefit of serving those meals to seniors is and what the impact of that benefit is. How are those meals helping you change the world?

So, your case must strive to talk about vision and impact. Yet that doesn't mean every case must be the same.

Based on your Asking Style, you're going to use a different vocabulary to describe your organization's vision and impact. You're going to tell a different story about those meals for seniors.

what's the goal?

EXTROVERT

what's the opportunity?

rainmaker

go-getter

ANALYTIC

INTUITIVE

what's the plan?

INTROVERT

what moves my heart?

mission controller

kindred spirit

Rainmakers will use facts and figures, outcomes, goals, and strategies to tell a story. You will tell a "goal story." Here's your Rainmaker version:

I'm so excited by our work with seniors at Allenville Senior Center. Our goal has been to decrease isolation and increase nutritional intake among seniors in our community so they have a better quality of life in their later years. By providing breakfast and lunch to seniors five days a week, we are impacting their lives in just a few weeks. Within a month of joining our Center, 75% of seniors self-report significant decreases in their feelings of isolation, and our registered nurse reports an almost complete elimination of the insidious weight loss these seniors often face when they're responsible for their own meals. One of our clients, Lucinda, self-reported that in the month she's been with us she has had significant decreases in her feelings of isolation, and she hasn't lost a single pound!

Go-Getters have the easiest time talking in a visionary way about the big picture possibilities, so building the case for support often comes easiest to you. Here's your "opportunity story."

I'm so excited by our work at Allenville Senior Center. Imagine what the world would be like if we could keep all seniors in society from any unnecessary decline in their later years. Well, here at Allenville we've come up with a solution for our community's seniors. By offering them breakfast and lunch every weekday, we've found it's possible to significantly decrease their feelings of isolation at the same time we get them all the nutrients they need to maintain their weight and their health. One of our clients, Lucinda, self-reported that in the month she's been with us she has had significant decreases in her feelings of isolation, and she hasn't lost a single pound! We're impacting lives such as Lucinda's in profound ways.

Kindred Spirits are more likely to talk about mission, weave in personal stories of program participants, or tell their own personal story. You'll tell a "heart story."

I'm so excited by our work at Allenville Senior Center and I'd like to share a story. Lucinda joined our senior center a month ago. When she first came, she was feeling completely isolated due to very limited human contact, and she was depressed that her life was so solitary. Living by herself, we also found she had been losing weight because she wasn't cooking well for herself and had regularly skipped meals. Obviously, her depression added to her lack of desire to eat. This is a story we hear time and again, and it breaks my heart to think these seniors—people's parents and grandparents—are in such dire straits. Since coming to Allenville, Lucinda has self-reported significant decreases in her feelings of isolation, and she hasn't lost a single pound. And this is true for the hundreds of seniors we serve every day.

Mission Controllers talk about methods, systems, and plans needed to have impact and fulfill the mission. Without a road-map, the end goal won't feel real to you. You'll tell a "plan story."

I'm so excited by our work at Allenville Senior Center, where we are directly addressing the issues of isolation and nutritional deficiency. We developed a program to identify at-risk seniors that includes home visits and check-ups. We enroll them at Allenville and a registered nurse does an intake to record their feelings of isolation, their weight, and other vitals. We then provide them breakfast and lunch five days a week. Through our work, 75% of seniors self-report significant decreases in their feelings of isolation, and our registered nurse reports an almost complete elimination of the insidious weight loss these seniors often face when they're responsible for their own meals. One of our clients, Lucinda, self-reported that in the month she's been with us she has had significant decreases in her feelings of isolation, and she hasn't lost a single pound!

EXERCISE: Create Your Story (20-30 minutes)

In my years of training, case for support has been the weakest link all around—for staff and volunteers alike. Creating your story takes practice. Creating a story that is focused on vision and impacts takes more practice. Try this at your next staff or board meeting:

- Break into groups of three
- Assign someone in each group to be the timer (on their phone)
- Round I: Each of the three makes a one-minute case for support with a focus on vision and impact (and the presenter must stop at one minute)
- The three debrief, talking about:
  - Who found it easier/harder to talk about vision and impact in their own words?
  - How did your Asking Style impact your case?
- Round II: Each of the three makes a one-minute case for support again
- The three debrief again
- The group reconvenes to share their experiences

Heads up... one minute is hard! And that's the point. Though you'll have a few minutes in the context of a meeting to make your case for support, you'll use your case much more often in more casual circumstances, and it will need to be more succinct.

Picture all those special events you attend—fundraisers, cultivation events, networking opportunities, etc. Often, you'll only have a minute or so to talk about your organization. It's not a lot of time, though if you use it well you'll make a great impression.

partnering

I'm a huge fan of partnering and I do so as often as possible. Asking with a partner can strengthen the ask in many ways, and for me it also makes asking more personally rewarding and enjoyable. I like having someone be part of the entire process with me, from strategizing and preparing to soliciting and following up. Each step of the way my partner strengthens the process.

Many permutations can work. The most important factor is relationship—each partner must have a separate, strategic relationship with the donor. As a director of development or executive director, I've partnered with other fundraising staff, program staff, and board members. I've been one of three staff on a visit, each with a different role and relationship.

I recall one meeting with five of us! It was during my tenure as Director of Development for the Midwest Region for my alma mater, Brandeis University. We were meeting with an alumnus and his wife, and the meeting included two other alumni who had been cultivating the donor, the president and vice president of the university, and me. We each had a role and a relationship.

Another factor for partnering is the Asking Styles.

The goal is to partner diagonally across the grid. Rainmakers and Kindred Spirits are a great pair, as are Mission Controllers and Go-Getters. By partnering diagonally, you are most likely to cover all the bases. If you want to ensure you've covered all the bases, choose partners with different Secondary Asking Styles as well.

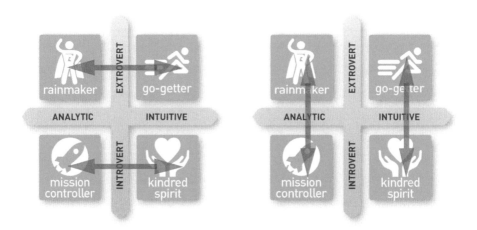

The ideal is to partner diagonally AND have different Secondary Asking Styles. Here are two examples:

RM/GG and KS/MC   ## MC/RM and GG/KS

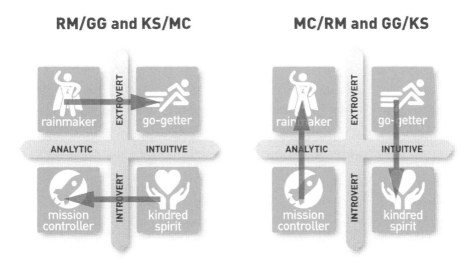

But never forget, the ideal is just that. It will be difficult to find your perfect match using the Asking Styles unless you have a large pool of askers. Don't let this stop you!

If you can't partner diagonally, try to have partners a) with different Primary Styles, and b) whose Styles don't overlap completely. For instance, if you're a Rainmaker/Mission Controller, a Mission Controller/Kindred Spirit would be fine:

Think back to presenting the case for support and let's use the Rainmaker as an example. If you're a Rainmaker you'll tell a "goal story." If you're telling that story to other Rainmakers, they'll not only find that story compelling because it's authentic to who you are, but they'll really appreciate it because you're speaking their language. Mission Controllers will also appreciate your authentic, analytic story, though they might then ask questions about how you plan to accomplish your goals. But what about Go-Getters and Kindred Spirits? Chances are they'll have lots of questions, even if their Secondary Asking Style is analytic (RM, MC).

Enter your Kindred Spirit partner, who's most likely to answer their questions satisfactorily after you make your case for support. And, if you happen to know your donor is a Kindred Spirit, perhaps your Kindred Spirit partner actually makes the case for support. We'll talk more about donors and their Styles in Chapter 11.

Now let's look at the extrovert/introvert dichotomy. By partnering with someone opposite from you on the interaction front, you will balance each other—and the meeting—out. I love soliciting gifts with an extrovert as I'm happy to let that person take the lead in the meeting.

Over 25 years, Ron Manderscheid (president of Northwestern Settlement House in Chicago) and I have been in more than a thousand meetings together. Ron's an extrovert (Go-Getter), and he's been wonderful at opening our meetings with donors while I get into my groove. He's also been more likely to talk a bunch while I, the introvert, have been happy to sit back and observe. This has given me the bandwidth to observe the meetings and move them ahead strategically. We always joke that Ron "goes long" and I have to rein him in. That sometimes has meant a kick under the table or some odd facial expression on my part, and sometimes it has meant saying "OK, Ron, we love hearing from you and can listen to you forever, but I'm watching the clock and we should move on from here. So-and-so doesn't have all day!" Take a look at Ron's version:

"Brian was my partner in asking for 25 years, and he taught me just about everything I know about fundraising. We each had our roles as we met with prospective donors. I talked about program—yes, sometimes too much! Brian was the asker. For the longest time I couldn't ask for an exact amount, and was lucky to have Brian by my side to do it. This recognition actually set our routine in leading up to each ask; I would say to the donor who I usually knew pretty well, 'while I am passionate about this program and love talking with you, it's very difficult for me to ask you about a financial gift...but Brian CAN.' It would always result in a good-humored chuckle, and provide a perfect segue for Brian to make the direct ask. The funny thing is that I never knew what he was going to request. We always decided on an amount in advance, but he would take the temperature of the meeting and sometimes ask for more or less. I would hold my breath every time! Together we raised more money than I ever could have imagined."

—*Ron Manderscheid*

Once you've chosen your partner, play to your strengths and understand what your partnership means dynamically. Let's say you're a Mission Controller and your best partner is a Kindred Spirit. You're both introverts, so think through how that might impact your meeting. Is your donor also introverted? That could make for a quiet meeting so identify a number of questions in advance and assume the meeting could still be shorter than longer. Are you a Rainmaker and Go-Getter—two extroverts? Make sure not to dominate the meeting. Who is going to be responsible for reining in the other?

determining the ask amount

Even when it comes to figuring out how much to request, our Asking Style will impact us. No question the Rainmakers will aim high. You're driven to get the biggest gifts and will feel the greatest sense of accomplishment if the gifts feel like "wins." You might even aim too high. Kindred Spirits will have to watch your tendency to aim low to avoid rejection. While your personal goal is often just to get a gift—any gift—the organization's goal is to get what represents a personally significant gift for the donor. Kindred Spirits and Rainmakers often complement each other well, often agreeing to an ask amount that's just right.

Go-Getters won't want to commit to an amount in advance—your comfort zone is to figure it out in the moment—but you must have one in mind before reaching out to set up the meeting, as we'll discuss later, and certainly in advance of a solicitation meeting.

Mission Controllers will want tons of information to inform your decision, and no matter how thorough the analysis you'll still be a bit unsure and not feel you're ready to move ahead. Go-Getters and Mission Controllers can be a challenging combination on this front as both hesitate to commit to a gift amount (though the Mission Controller is more likely to commit because it's part of the plan and must be completed!)

> **TIP:**
>
> **Past giving is often not a good indication of future giving so don't rely on formulas. Instead, take the time to learn everything you can about each donor. and then ask for personally significant gifts. Don't worry about asking for "too little." If your donor responds quickly and seemingly without much thought, you now have more information and will ask for significantly more next time.**

role plays
strategy sessions
rainmaker

EXTROVERT

go-getter
role plays
talking with others

ANALYTIC   INTUITIVE

structured practice
script
mission
controller

INTROVERT

kindred
spirit
one-on-one practice
notes and questions

practice

Please don't wing the meeting and, yes, I'm talking to you Go-Getters first and foremost! I know you're not big on practice—you have confidence in your intuition and you're so comfortable with people generally you think you can handle the job. Yet practice will help you stay on point, make a more cohesive case for support, and run a more strategic and accomplished meeting. Practice, and overall preparation, will make a huge difference.

Practice comes in many forms. Rainmakers will naturally be most strategic. You'll spend the most time figuring out how to conduct the meeting in a way that most engages your donors and gets them to share what they're thinking and feeling. Go-Getters won't be this strategic, but if you've got an opportunity to role play with others you'll enjoy the interactive and quick-on-your-feet nature of the activity.

Kindred Spirits will be much more comfortable having a general discussion about the donor with your asking partner and taking some notes to review before the meeting. Mission Controllers will be particularly drawn to structured one-on-one practices and are most likely to write out a script to serve as your guide.

If you're looking for a role play for your next training, I find this is one is incredibly effective:

SOLICITOR ROUND-ROBIN (15-20 minutes)

- Best in groups of three
- Figure out who will be the solicitor, the donor, and the observer
- The solicitor asks five questions about the donor's philanthropy and relationship to the organization, such as:
  - How do you decide which organizations to support?
  - What is it about our organization that matters most to you?
  - What would you most like to know about us?
- The solicitor asks the donor for $5,000 for the annual fund
- The donor says he'll consider it and asks a few questions
- The solicitor tries to find out what might move the donor to a decision
- The donor and solicitor agree on next steps
- The observer comments on how effective the solicitor was at:
  - Engaging the donor
  - Learning about the donor
  - Moving the donor further toward "yes".
- Note: If you have the time, have people switch roles and repeat the exercise.

---

eight

---

how each style sets up the meeting

 If you can get the meeting you can almost always get a gift—some gift of some amount for some project at some time. It doesn't mean you'll get exactly what you hoped for when you hoped for it, but very few people will meet with you just to give you an unequivocal no—"I won't give you anything, ever, for anything. Go away. Do not come back. Do not pass 'Go.' Do not collect $200."

Here's the kicker. This is only the case if you're upfront about why you want to meet. Never say "I'd like to pick your brain" or "I'd like to get to know you better" when what you want to do is ask for a gift. Say "I'd like to meet with you to ask you for a gift to the library. Would you consider meeting with me at your convenience?"

Yes, you will be rejected for meetings, but wouldn't you rather be rejected for a meeting than in a meeting? Further, and more importantly, if you meet with a donor under false pretenses you will damage the relationship. No donor likes having a one-two pulled on him.

People often worry not only about being rejected, but that donors might feel you asked for a gift too early in the relationship. Keep in mind some prospects need lots of cultivation before making a gift. Some are happy to do so the first time you meet. If you're not sure if your prospect is ready, ask her if she is rather than assuming so—"I know you're just getting to know our organization this year but I didn't want to assume you wouldn't want to contribute yet. Does it feel like the right timing or would you like to get to know us better first?"

> **TIP:**
>
> ------
>
> If you have to call a donor rather than write and you're anxious about doing so, make the call early in the day. Getting your most difficult task out of the way early helps it from becoming more daunting as the day goes on. And you'll have a great sense of accomplishment going forward.

Since it's important to be clear and upfront, you need to ask yourself how you're going to reach out in a way that allows you to do that. I've heard people say you must pick up the phone, and to them I say hogwash. I wouldn't have agreed 20 years ago, and I certainly wouldn't agree now. First of all, it's hard to reach people by phone these days. If people have a home phone, they're generally not there to answer it and, if they're home, might see your call as an intrusion. If they only have a cell phone, do you know your donors well enough to reach them that way? Or will it feel like you've overstepped your bounds?

Second, if you really dislike the phone for one reason or another, chances are you're not going to do your best job over the phone. Re-member that you have to be prepared to deal with a variety of situa-tions including the donor picking up the phone only to say he doesn't have time to talk or asking you to be quick. Or you might reach another family member who has no idea who you are and is suspicious of the call. This is all to say the phone is not the be-all and endall. It's one of many options. So, use it if it suits who you are and makes sense given the donor. Let the Asking Styles be your guide.

Go-Getters are most likely to just pick up the phone when the mood strikes. You're comfortable jumping into the conversation that way and you're at ease dealing with the various challenges the phone brings. I've always been amazed how easily my Settlement boss and asking partner, Ron, picks up the phone to call donors (often with me sitting there with my Secondary Mission Controller hat on to keep him moving forward in an organized fashion).

Not so for a Kindred Spirit. If you're like me, you'll write as often as you can—usually emails these days but sometimes a letter saying you'll fol-low up by phone. The email/letter lets you make your case for meeting fully (including a bit of your case for support) without being cut off and having to think quickly on your feet. And when your donor responds by email, you get to digest what she's said before responding again. As a "think to talk" introvert, this follows your thought patterns well.

Mission Controllers also prefer writing first, but for you it's not only about thinking to talk but also about having the opportunity to be systematic and methodical in the way you present your case. You want to lay it out clearly and in detail, and an email/letter lets you make the case fully and cohesively.

Rainmakers will be most strategic about whether you use the phone, email, or a letter. The decision might be based on the relationship, on what you know about the donor, on past interactions, or what's practical.

One caveat here. Sometimes you have to switch methods. You can't keep calling or writing if you're not getting a response. As much as I love email, if I've tried by email a number of times without response, I will pick up the phone. At the end of the day our job is to reach our donors, and it's better to reach them imperfectly than not to reach them at all.

nine

how each style asks for the gift

Now the moment has arrived. You and your donor are meeting to talk about a gift to your organization.

Most important is to understand that this meeting is an intentional conversation. If you haven't planned it out and identified your intentions, you will accomplish far less. While soliciting a gift is an important intention, it's not the only one. Even in an ask meeting, building the relationship is paramount. It's more important than the gift. Why is that?

The beauty of individual donors is their loyalty. Institutional funders aren't driven by loyalty, but by their own mission, guidelines, and leadership desires (staff and board). And this means their funding priorities invariably change over time. Foundations, even if their priorities are consistent, don't want organizations dependent on them, so they often have policies such as "three years on and one year off," or "we don't make general operating grants." Corporations are always in flux—merging, being bought out, having changes in leadership—and way too often take a year off in the process to contemplate the future. Government funding has a host of other challenges.

Individuals, however, tend to give for long periods of time—often forever—and with far fewer expectations. Think of your own philanthropy. If someone pays attention to you, acknowledges your gifts, and keeps you posted on the successes of the organization, you'll keep giving...and often in increasing amounts. And the better you know an organization the more likely you are to trust it enough to make unrestricted gifts—gifts that go to the bottom line to keep the organization strong. Your giving is based on relationships and over time your loyalty builds as the relationships grow. Further, you feel a personal sense of responsibility to those you're assisting, a responsibility to come through, as you know others are dependent on you.

> TIP:
> _____
>
> Listening is key. The more you listen the more you'll learn. As Jerry Panas would say, "no one's ever listened their way out of a gift!"

Given this, the goal is to build a deep relationship with an individual donor that leadS to an annuity of gifts over the donor's lifetime. And that means the relationship always comes before the gift.

those opening moments

As an introvert, I always find the first few minutes of a solicitation meeting challenging. In fact, I find the first few minutes of any meeting or gathering challenging. I need those first moments to gather my thoughts, get a read on the other participants, and become accustomed to the environment.

If I know a donor well, that's helpful, as I have a better sense of what to expect from our interaction. More often than not, as I discussed earlier, I'm soliciting someone I don't know particularly well, and that creates some anxiety. Ideally, I've brought along an extroverted asking partner (Rainmaker or Go-Getter) who can get the meeting started while I sit back and get more comfortable.

> TIP:
> _____
> This is for everyone, but particularly introverts. Take the time to write out a handful of personal questions to ask at the top of the meeting. Though you won't be able to reference the list (can you imagine reading your questions from a list?), just writing the questions down in advance will help you recall them at the time. I probably don't even have to recommend this to you Mission Controllers as you'll have scripted things out as part of your meeting preparation.

exploring

A well-run meeting is full of exploration. In addition to the opening personal questions, much time is spent exploring your donor's relationship to the organization and to philanthropy. What does the donor think of your organization? Are there particular programs he finds most appealing? What is he trying to accomplish philanthropically? If he's given before, what prompted those gifts and how does he feel about having made them?

> "As a Mission Controller, I think one of my strengths is as a listener. And I think I'm very good at drawing people out and getting to know them, in a way that's not necessarily goal-oriented in terms of the gift but in terms of the relationship. I'm very research-oriented and detail-oriented. I want to know the backstory before I go talk to someone. I'm slower, more methodical and more likely to let something evolve rather than push for speed. I try to listen for the natural pace of something. As it needs to be for a donor."
>
> —*Lisa Metcalf, Arts Management Consultant*

No matter how well we know donors—and we often don't know them well—we learn much during our exploration. In fact, it's during our exploration that we find out not only why they give or would give, but what would encourage them to give more. Do you know what would encourage your donors to give their biggest gifts to your organization? Don't make the mistake of thinking your donors come to meetings set on a gift level and you can't influence their decisions. You can make an impact if you can tap into what would inspire them to give more. Take a look below for a quick exercise that underscores this point.

EXERCISE: Hi-Low (15 minutes)

1. Either break into groups or discuss as a whole. Think of an organization you plan to support this year (perhaps one you support every year)

2. What is the least you will contribute to it this year?

3. What is the most you can imagine giving that organization this year?

4. What would make the difference? If in groups, reconvene to discuss.

I bet you'll be surprised by the range. The last time I did this myself the largest gift I would have considered was five times what I gave. And what would have made the difference for me? If a particular person had asked me face-to-face!

After we ask for a gift we have further opportunities for exploration, this time as we try to fully understand a donor's immediate reaction to the request. What more would she like to know? What excites her about the organization? What might get in the way of making a gift?

As with every step of the asking process your Asking Style will impact how you go about these explorations. Now, my fellow Kindred Spirits might be thinking, "oh no—I've got to ask all these questions? That feels so intrusive."

Well, here's the good news... it is much better to talk less and listen more—much more! My motto is, "ask short questions and hope for long answers." The less you talk and the more you listen, the more you'll learn. And that's key to every interaction with a donor, including a solicitation meeting. So, while my fellow Kindred Spirits do need to ask questions, the explorations put the donors front and center.

> **TIP:**
>
> There's no such thing as a perfect ask and that shouldn't be your goal. You'll always walk away wishing you did something different – talked less, asked a different question, moved the meeting along at a different pace. So what?!

Mission Controllers and Go-Getters find exploration easier. Chances are you Mission Controllers have an outline, a script, a list of questions, or some other framework, and you're very happy to systematically move through your questions, sitting back quietly in between. Go-Getters, having a natural curiosity about others, find it easy to sprinkle the conversation with questions, though their questions might wander.

Rainmakers aren't big on process, so they won't naturally ask a lot of questions. However, the questions they do ask will be strategically posed. They'll ask the questions that are most relevant and revealing.

getting the words out

I always say there are three moments in the asking process that are most difficult. The first, as we discussed earlier, is reaching out to set up the solicitation meeting, as this is the first instance you might face resistance or outright rejection.

The second of the most difficult moments is asking for the gift. Some fundraisers get so anxious at this moment they let the meeting go by without having asked! Even the best fundraisers can be challenged at this moment.

The ideal time to ask for the gift is somewhere in the middle of the meeting, after much exploration about the donor's relationship to the organization and philanthropy, but not so late in the meeting there won't be time to explore the donor's response to your request. Sensing when that moment has arrived is challenging. And even if it feels like the right time, how do you segue to this moment, which involves acknowledging what you've learned and making your personal case for support? It can feel like an abrupt change of course.

What's your challenge at this critical moment? If you're a Rainmaker, you might have the urge to "close" too quickly. You're not a big process person, so after asking your donor a couple of questions and answering a few of theirs, you're probably thinking, "OK, can we just get to the meat and potatoes?" Always remember this is about building a relationship, and the more time you spend exploring and learning about your donor, the more you'll build the relationship. What other questions might you ask? Have you asked your donor if she has other questions?

Ron and his fellow Go-Getters will resist closing. I know what you're thinking—"we're having such a lovely conversation... why ruin it by asking for a gift?" Now this assumes you're even aware it's time to segue to your case for support. Just as likely, you're so in the moment, so wrapped up in the conversation, you forget to move on. Go-Getters—never forget solicitations are business meetings, and it's your role to move them along to make certain you cover the full agenda.

My fellow Kindred Spirits will relate to my general sense of anxiety at this moment, which comes from our issues with confrontation. Now of course this isn't a confrontational moment, but since we take everything personally we can mistakenly see it that way. In our attempt to avoid confrontation, we'll have a tendency to stall as long as possible.

Last, a word for you Mission Controllers. Yes, an ask should generally come about halfway through a solicitation meeting. But some meetings are so rich in conversation it makes sense to extend the exploration. Other times it's like pulling teeth to get your donor to talk and you may very well find yourself out of questions early on. Don't be completely beholden to the system and be certain to treat each meeting as a unique conversation that has its own rhythm and timing.

post-ask: the third most difficult moment

As challenging as it can be to ask for the gift (and at the right time), it's often just as challenging to keep silent after you've asked. Those five seconds—it's rarely more than that—can feel like an eternity, right? This moment reminds me of when a check comes to the table at the end of a donor meeting. Our hope is the donor will pick it up, seeing it as part of their support of the institution. But you can only wait five seconds before grabbing the check yourself.

Here's where the Mission Controller's love of following instructions comes in handy. If you've been taught that being silent until the donor talks is best practice, you'll gladly follow that guideline. Also, as the best listener in the group, you'll be glad your time to talk is over and you can now sit back and listen.

Rainmakers will want to fill the silence by sharing more facts. Go-Getters will see the silence as a conversation killer and try to fill it with the first thing that comes to mind. Kindred Spirits will be relieved they've gotten the ask out, but might keep talking if they're anxious.

TIP:

For 30 years my number one prop has been a beverage. I make every effort to have something to drink—even just a cup of water—by my side. As soon as I've asked the donor to consider a particular gift, I lift up the glass and take a sip. Try it now. It takes about five seconds to reach for it, pick it up, take a sip, and put it back down. Virtually every time, in those five seconds, your donor will respond. Remember, you're having a conversation. It's in the hands of the donor to respond... however long it takes and however many sips you need to take!

ten

how each style follows through

What happens after a solicitation meeting is critical to successfully closing gifts and building relationships. From an immediate and personal thank you for the meeting to continued cultivation throughout the year, this is not the time to coast. The renewal rates in our industry are abysmal—overall only 46% of all 2015 donors renewed their gifts the following year—and so I can't stress enough just how critical follow-through is.

As with every step of the asking process, we have core strengths. Some of us will be amazing at continuously developing relationships through personalized contact. Some of us will excel at writing up contact reports and keeping the major gift tracker current. Yet others will be great at always keeping their donors in mind.

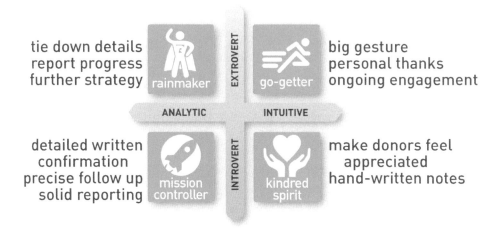

tie down details
report progress
further strategy — **rainmaker**

EXTROVERT

go-getter — big gesture
personal thanks
ongoing engagement

ANALYTIC   **INTUITIVE**

detailed written
confirmation
precise follow up
solid reporting — **mission controller**

INTROVERT

kindred spirit — make donors feel
appreciated
hand-written notes

Rainmakers can be counted on to tie down details after a meeting. Your drive and focus keep you from letting things fall through the cracks and you will keep after a donor until the gift is signed, sealed, and delivered. In fact, you might be challenged to show the necessary patience as the donor's decision process unfolds. You're also very helpful developing ongoing strategies for that donor.

Yet, at the end of the day, you'd still prefer to move onto the next "sale." Your excitement comes from reaching your numeric goals, and closing another gift gets you closer to those goals in the short run. Also, you're not big on process, and ongoing cultivation doesn't keep you revved up. In fact, some donors will frustrate you with their requests for attention, information and involvement.

My most important advice to you is not to abandon your current donors in favor of new prospects. While getting gifts from new prospects is exciting and gives you a sense of short-term accomplishment, we know nothing is more important than the annuity of gifts from a donor you cultivate year-in and year-out. If you stick with your donors you'll accomplish so much more in the long-term. Most game-changing gifts come from those who have given to our organizations regularly over time.

If you're really struggling with the process of cultivation, is there anyone on your team who can help? Perhaps it's a Mission Controller, who will frame out a cultivation plan and make sure it gets accomplished. Or perhaps it's a Go-Getter, who will enjoy those interactions.

 Go-Getters knock it out of the park on the relationship side. You're great at warmly, enthusiastically, and personally thanking your donors, and your love of people leads you to want to stay in touch. Your innate curiosity helps you get to know them well and to understand what motivates their philanthropy. This relationship brings them closer to the organization as well. In fact, some become your friends—part of your "one big happy family".

However, you're not always the most strategic about follow-up and follow-through. You know you need to keep after a donor until the gift is closed, but you tend to be laid back, checking in here and there. It will be hard to structure the follow-up so you have an agreed-to expectation as to when the donor will respond and, hopefully, commit.

In your on-going engagement, you're great at in-the-moment gestures. Yet they aren't always thought through as part of a larger plan, which can be difficult for you to develop. So while a donor might take kindly to the individual gestures, they, might not be in the best long-term interest of the relationship and the organization.

And your relationships risk crossing the line, where they become more personal than professional. If you sense you're beginning to struggle with a relationship for this very reason, consider partnering with a Rainmaker or Mission Controller. Their objectivity will help recalibrate the relationship and they'll be able to help you think through donor cultivation activity more strategically and systematically. Don't lean on us Kindred Spirits—we'll just reinforce those subjective tendencies!

Kindred Spirits are wonderful at helping donors feel appreciated. Your attentive and caring nature helps nurture donor relationships as you're always wondering what you can do for your donors to make them feel valued. And I always say if anyone is going to write a handwritten thank you note a Kindred Spirit will (but not me—I have the handwriting of a first grader and it's simply too mortifying to use it).

Kindred Spirits have two key challenges. First, you're cautious about following up to close gifts. You're concerned that you might be haranguing donors and it becomes awkward for you when you can't get their attention. But you must remember, if you don't continue to follow up you risk giving the impression your donors' gifts aren't important. So keep at it!

Second, you have a tendency to focus on all donors regardless of whether it makes sense strategically. You tend to want to give everyone a lot of attention, and it's hard for you to accept the fact that you should be paying more attention to your largest donors...or that some people you're in touch with probably shouldn't get any attention as they won't become major gift donors no matter what you do.

Your best partner will be a Rainmaker. Imagine if you partnered with a Rainmaker who could follow up to close gifts and who could also help you be more strategic about your portfolio of donors.

> **TIP:**
>
> Do you (Go-Getters in particular) hate writing contact reports? Use Voice Memo or another app on your phone to dictate what you've learned, and then copy/paste it into a report when you're back at your desk. You'll have to edit it a bit, but you'll be 90% of the way there.

Where would we be without Mission Controllers, as no one does their job more fastidiously. You follow every step, you write up fantastic notes and contact reports, and you continue to work through the process to make sure nothing falls through the cracks. You will methodically follow up with your donors at agreed-to times until they've made a firm decision one way or another.

You excel at systematically keeping your major gift tracker up to date, so no one gets forgotten, and you make sure donors get regular attention. Once you've calendared your cultivation steps, it becomes easy to get them done. Your work helps carry everyone on your team forward.

So, can you guess what trips up Mission Controllers? In a business that's focused on relationships, where everyone needs to be treated individually, you have a tendency to be too methodical. For example, the copy/paste function is your friend, so keep in mind that no matter how similar thank you letters and other correspondence might seem, each one is an opportunity to communicate directly and uniquely with one donor.

Your best partners will be Go-Getters and Kindred Spirits. They'll complement your thorough efforts with their personal touch.

eleven

---

seeing your donors through the asking styles lens

You may notice that I've referred to donors' Asking Styles in this book. Of course, in the context of our fundraising they're not the askers—we are. However, we can use the Asking Styles as a framework for understanding how to best work with them.

figuring out your donor's asking style

How do you figure out your donor's Asking Style? If you have never met your donor, you can make an educated guess.

Perhaps you look at career. Lawyers are generally analytics, often Mission Controllers. Think of what it takes to learn the law, research cases, write briefs, etc. Artists are often intuitives. They've got a vision and express it artistically. If they need to share that vision with others, perhaps they're Go-Getters. People who run companies could be Rainmakers, as drive and strategic thinking are key assets for them. Those who work in helping professions—nurses, therapists, etc.—could be Kindred Spirits.

You might also look at how your donor prefers to communicate. Is it always by phone (Go-Getter) or always by email (Mission Controller or Kindred Spirit)? Is she formal (Mission Controller) or informal (Go-Getter)? Does she ask you a lot of questions (Rainmaker) or not (Kindred Spirit)?

If you've met your donor you've got more to go on. You now have a sense of the types of questions she asks and the type (and quantity) of material she requests. An analytic will ask for facts, figures, statistics, reports, plans, etc. An intuitive will ask you to share program and participant stories. You know whether a donor's quieter (introvert) or more talkative (extrovert). You know how much personal information she likes to share. Go-Getters and Kindred Spirits will share more than their analytic counterparts.

Once you've got a sense of your donors' Asking Styles, you can anticipate their needs, the questions they'll ask, how they might conduct themselves in meetings, and more.

Here's a quick exercise for you and your fellow staff or volunteers:

EXERCISE: What Are Your Donor's Styles? (20 minutes)

- Make a list of 10 donors everyone in your group has met
- Ask everyone to guess the 10 donors' Asking Styles (maybe even Primary and Secondary?)
- Compare notes and discuss

what your donors will be interested in learning

Though there's no question you need to lead with your passion and authenticity, and that means making a case for support based on what excites you about your organization, it's also true that you should do your best to provide the information your donors request. In most cases they'll simply ask for it.

If you're a Rainmaker talking about the goals and outcomes of the organization, your Kindred Spirit donor might respond by saying, "thank you for sharing that with me. Do you have any specific examples of a patient who was helped through that therapy?" If you're a Go-Getter waxing poetic about your organization's vision and the opportunity it has to make an impact, your Mission Controller donor might say, "That's so exciting to hear. How do you plan to make the most of that opportunity?"

The goal is to think through the meeting in advance and plan for some of these moments, and understanding your donor's Asking Style can help you work through various scenarios. Of course, if you and your donor share an Asking Style, you're probably in good shape already. If you're both intuitives or analytics, you'll be on a similar path. But what if you're not?

Let's say you're a Kindred Spirit and your donor is a Rainmaker. Now you know to ask the program staff to provide you with their outcomes measurements. And you might bring the executive summary for your strategic plan and take a moment to scan it before the meeting.

What if you're a Mission Controller and your donor is a Kindred Spirit? Take some time to meet with program staff and ask them to provide you with a few heartwarming stories of participants whose lives have been impacted by your organization. Perhaps the staff will even write out a few that you can bring to the meeting.

While your donor's sweet spot might never be yours, it doesn't mean you don't make an effort to hear her and provide what she wants. And let's never forget that it's perfectly fine not to have all the answers in the moment, offering instead to find and share them afterward.

how they'll interact in the meeting

The introvert/extrovert dichotomy is very telling. Two extroverts will certainly have a lively conversation, though you will still need to be sure to leave your donor the space to dominate the conversation. If you're both introverts the meeting might be quieter, and the challenge could be finding ways to ensure your donor dominates the conversation.

Rainmaker donors will be laser-focused and ask strategic and sometimes challenging questions. It will be important not to internalize those challenges and understand it's part of the Rainmaker's nature to fire away questions.

Go-Getter donors will be high-energy and enthusiastic, and you'll learn a lot about them. However, they might unwittingly throw the meeting off track with unrelated questions and topics. You might have to work to keep the meeting organized and moving ahead.

Kindred Spirit donors will be focused on how they can help you and your organization, and they'll be congenial and nonconfrontational. This means they're unlikely to ask the questions on their minds and it will be your job to coax them out. Otherwise the donors will leave the meeting ultimately unfulfilled.

Mission Controller donors will appreciate well-structured meetings where they can clearly see the path you're taking and can easily follow along. If they're not sure where a meeting is headed they'll be thrown, so it will be helpful to be transparent as you move meetings along. By their nature Mission Controllers will speak the least, so it will be important to come prepared with lots of questions to ask along the way.

how likely are they to commit in the moment?

Who do you think will be most likely to commit right on the spot? I believe it's the Kindred Spirit, because she is wired to come through for others and act selflessly and will feel a sense of responsibility to commit right then and there.

You're least likely to get a firm commitment from a Mission Controller, who will want to review everything in detail, gather more information independently, and then systematically and analytically figure out what the best response would be. Of course, even after all that there will be hesitation as there is always more information for a Mission Controller to glean.

A Rainmaker will also want to take a moment to think about the request and the strategic value of her gift, and therefore might want more information and time to analyze the situation. However, she will appreciate your goal of closing gifts and reaching a fundraising goal, and she'll want to be part of that effort.

The Go-Getter will be very enthusiastic, possibly getting swept up in the moment. However, as a process person she might put off the decision to think about it from various angles.

working with two or more donors

I always encourage donors to bring their spouses, partners, adult children, or anyone else who would ultimately influence their decision. It's important to meet them early in the relationship to understand their agendas, which don't always align completely with the donors' agendas. We also get to see the family dynamic at play, which can be very revealing. While these meetings are fruitful, they can also be more difficult to manage as there are now three relationships at work simultaneously—you and donor No. 1, you and donor No. 2, and donors No. 1 and No. 2.

When one of the donors is extroverted and the other is introverted, the extrovert will generally ask and answer more questions, and it will be your job to ask the introvert questions. Otherwise you risk the introvert leaving the meeting feeling ignored. You can also ask a question where the answer would be unique to each of them and request they both answer it. How about "Can each of you remember when you made your first charitable gift? How did that feel?"

Perhaps one donor is analytic and the other intuitive. If you're analytic, you and the analytic donor might bond more quickly as you'll be speaking the same language and you'll be able to answer her questions more fully. If you're analytic and they're both intuitive, you'll have to work to overcome the subconscious feeling that they're speaking one language and you're speaking another.

How about if one donor is a Mission Controller and one is a Go-Getter? The Mission Controller will appreciate an organized, linear meeting, yet the Go-Getter will send the meeting in various directions. How will you work to attain a happy medium?

Whenever there are three or more of you in a meeting together, whatever the permutations, use some of your preparation time to chart out the likely dynamics based on everyone's Asking Style. Developing a sense of how the meeting will unfold will be that much more important than in a one-on-one meeting. When you're only dealing with one donor, as the meeting unfolds you can get a read, take her lead, and see a clear path forward. That will be harder as you try to engage two donors at once.

twelve

working as a team

The Asking Styles are a powerful framework for figuring out how to build the strongest asking team at your organization. No one is strong in every facet of any business, and fundraising is no exception. The key to success in business is to build a strong team, a team in which every member brings his or her unique skillset to the table and is honored and respected for those skills.

In Chapter 7 we discussed partnering on asks, where a blend of Asking Styles can lead to a stronger solicitation. Your ideal partner through the

Asking Styles lens is someone diagonal to you; Rainmakers and Kindred Spirits complement each other, as do Go-Getters and Mission Controllers. And those of adjacent Styles can also be a strong team, as long as your Primary and Secondary Asking Styles don't overlap completely.

Now, let's look at your entire asking team, and not just through the lens of the ask itself, but through everything it takes to run a major gift program (meaning face-to-face asking). Who's on your team? If you're a mid-sized shop, your team might consist of an executive director, a director of development, and a major gift officer (and perhaps many gift officers if you're a larger institution). What are the Asking Styles of your team and how does that impact your work?

Let's assume an executive director, Arlene, is a Go-Getter; her director of development, Brenda, is a Mission Controller; and their major gift officer, Robert, is a Kindred Spirit.

What are the strengths and challenges of your team and how might you address them?

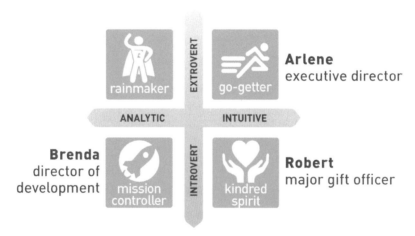

You've got Executive Director Arlene (GG) who is outgoing and is great at engaging people and talking in a visionary and exciting way. You've got Director of Development Brenda (MC) who excels at developing the asking plan, keeping it moving along, and preparing meticulously for meetings. They can be a potent asking team as their Styles are diagonal from each other, and Brenda (MC) can be counted on to keep Arlene (GG) on track and getting out the door to see the right people. I can imagine Brenda excelling at sitting with Arlene in Arlene's office while Arlene calls donors to set up meetings for the two of them, as I did all those years with my buddy Ron. And boy, will Brenda (MC) appreciate that since she won't want to make those calls!

Yet Arlene (GG) might frustrate Brenda (MC) to no end because it's likely she won't al-ways make the calls Brenda wants her to, and while she will win people over in meet-ings with her pas-sion for the vision, it will be hard to keep her on message and keep her from talk-ing too much and not listening enough. It  will be imperative for Brenda to plan practice sessions—probably with role playing—before meetings.

Brenda (MC) might frustrate Arlene (GG) as well by not fully em-bracing all the plans for program growth. In Brenda's eyes, Arlene can get ahead of herself, building new programs when other pro-grams still need more funding. In a related scenario, Brenda might find Arlene unreasonable in the goals she sets out for fundraising. Brenda is likely to be more conservative in those plans as she dots her i's and crosses her t's and will want to have great certainty any plan will work.

How about the relationship between Director of Development Bren-da (MC) and Major Gift Officer Robert (KS)? As partners on asks, these two introverts will need to plan meticulously to make sure they've iden-

tified many questions to ask. Brenda can be charged with systematically keeping the meeting going while Robert will use his intuition to
sense when the conversation has reached the magic moment when
it's time to present the case for support and ask for the gift.

Back in the office, Brenda (MC) and Robert (KS) will work closely day
in and day out. While these introverts won't talk over each other, they
also might be reticent to speak honestly and openly about issues that
have arisen. This will be particularly true for Robert as a Kindred Spirit
and the subordinate. His boss, Brenda, will have to make an effort to
create a trusting environment and an objective system for feedback
and review.

Brenda (MC) will need to understand that Robert (KS) won't always be as organized and methodical as she is. Also, while Brenda
will crave detailed contact reports, a tracker that's up-to-date, and
other reporting mechanisms, Robert might struggle on this front,
especially if his Secondary Asking Style is Go-Getter and he's a pure
intuitive.

Along these lines, Brenda (MC) will create detailed plans for the
department, and these will prove hard for Robert (KS) to follow (again
even more so if his Secondary Asking Style is Go-Getter). Brenda will
need to give Robert leeway to get the job done in his own way. As a
Kindred Spirit I can clearly recall my challenges in this area, and I suc-
ceeded most when my bosses were willing to give me the space to do
my job in my own comfortable way.

Good teamwork is built on mutual respect and admiration. No one
on your team will be strong in everything they do (including you!). When
you understand each other's Asking Style and embrace everyone for
the great set of skills they do possess, you'll be the strongest fundraising team possible.

EXERCISE #1: Asking and the Styles (20-30 minutes)

- Have everyone take the Asking Style Assessment

- Break into pairs to discuss the following questions:

  - If we partnered on a solicitation, how would we work together?

  - If one of us were the solicitor and one the donor, how would we interact?

- Reconvene to discuss

EXERCISE #2: Work Dynamics (30-45 minutes)

- Have everyone take the Asking Style Assessment

- Break into pairs to discuss the following questions:

  - What would our Styles mean for how we'd interact in staff meetings?

  - If one of you reported to the other, how would your Asking Styles impact that relationship? What if the positions were reversed?

- Reconvene to discuss

thirteen

---

working with your board

---

board involvement in fundraising is critical. Period.

It wasn't always the case. Back in the 70s and even 80s, many organizations got by with modest board involvement. Personal giving, except for the largest nonprofits, was often insignificant, and board job descriptions were rather vague on the topic of "giving and getting." Foundation money was easier to obtain and more of it was for general operating support. Corporations had pure philanthropic arms and their foundation directors had the autonomy to go out into the community and spread the wealth, which meant the little guy got a share. Government contracts weren't punitive.

Today the institutional sources are all problematic in one way or another (I could write a treatise on that topic!). Even if they weren't, the fact is institutional gifts are a small piece of the pie. As I noted in Chapter 1, of all charitable gifts (government sources not included), only 14% came from corporations and large foundations in 2017. Almost 87% came from individuals—70% outright, 9% through bequests, and 16% from small family foundations.

While staff is often capable of cultivating and stewarding institutional donors with modest help from the board (for their connections and participation in site visits), staff cannot handle individuals on their own. There are simply too many individuals to deal with and they require individualized attention. Let's not forget that 80% of all nonprofits have annual budgets of less than $1 million, and 60% exist on less than $250,000. On such small budgets there might not be any fundraising staff and all fundraising responsibility will fall to the executive director, who is wearing 50 hats. Even with one fulltime fundraiser, only a sliver of time can be spent cultivating and soliciting individuals.

Individual fundraising means all hands on deck—and the impact is extraordinary when that happens. Let's say you've got a board of 15 to 20. If each board member assists with four prospects, that's 60 to 80 individuals being cultivated, asked, thanked, and stewarded. Wow!

boards and the asking styles

The Asking Styles are an even more important lens for the board. A great number of board members are sitting on their first board. Even if they have prior board experience, chances are most of the fundraising they've been asked to do to date has been inviting friends, family, and associates to special events and writing end-of-year appeal letters. I can guarantee you most have never cultivated individuals, not to mention asked them face-to-face for a significant gift.

Adding to this, most board members come to your organization wishing they could do anything other than fundraise because they assume—and organizations often reinforce this—that their role is to "hit up" everyone they know. To turn over their contact lists, to send invitations broadly, and to generally partcipate in the deadly quid pro quo. They assume fundraising is going to be akin to a root canal—it's incredibly painful but they'll have to do it. Oh, and on top of that we give them virtually no training and then send them out to slaughter. Oy vey!

Yet it doesn't have to be this way. Though fundraising for most board members will always be a challenge, it can come to feel doable and even rewarding. Enter the Asking Styles.

board training

Let's start by talking about training. In Chapter 7 we talked about the need to practice—not only for the meeting itself but also for setting up the meeting if by phone. Yet that all assumes training, of which your board has had very little, if any. Board members must have training if they're going to be involved in cultivating and soliciting donors.

Training involves helping them understand their mindset, their strengths and challenges, and best practices. Training is an opportunity to discuss their fears and put them in perspective. And, perhaps most importantly, it's an opportunity to develop their personal story—their case for support.

If staff members are challenged to develop a strong, authentic personal case for support, imagine how challenging it is for board members. Board members generally feel they don't know enough about the organization to be articulate with others. They're afraid they'll say the wrong thing or be asked questions they can't answer.

Helping board members develop their case for support based on their Asking Style will alleviate their anxiety and help them feel empowered. It will help them understand the power of being authentic to their own experience and perspective, and get them past the notion that they need to know everything about your organization in order to be great ambassadors for it.

Over the years, as I've worked with board members from hundreds of organizations, I've seen them blossom before my eyes once they've come to understand how to use their own personality to make a strong case for support. There's a collective sigh of relief when they find out they don't need to be experts on everything their organizations do.

EXERCISE: Board Member Stories (20-30 minutes)

- Ask everyone to write down a 100-word answer to this request: "Tell me about your organization?"

- Have everyone read their answer aloud.

- Discuss what people liked about each other's stories and how their stories reflected their Asking Styles.

---

board member prospects

As you move away from the deadening quid pro quo and involve your board members in more strategic fundraising, the Asking Styles will be their roadmap in choosing prospects to cultivate and help solicit. As we noted in Chapter 6, staff—especially major gift officers—often have portfolios, and may have less flexibility in whom they cultivate and solicit. Not true for board members. Board members should cultivate and solicit those with whom they're comfortable and can feel confident. It's the only way to make their work palatable and keep their anxiety to a minimum. The only way to ensure they'll be successful.

Some board members will be fine reaching out to friends and family, in particular Mission Controllers and Go-Getters. Your extroverted board members—the Rainmakers and Go-Getters—will enjoy opening the door to new prospects. Rainmakers will be the best at strategically working their professional contacts. Mission Controllers will be happy dealing with the organization's family foundation prospects and can be particularly helpful with other institutional funders should that need exist.

preparing to ask

The Asking Styles will also inform how you prepare board members. Gone are the days of providing all board members with massive binders or email folders of identical material about the organization and their prospects. More is not always more! Your Mission Controller (and Rainmaker) board members will appreciate all that detail, but your Go-Getters and Kindred Spirits will become anxious at the thought of reviewing so much information—and it might stop them from reading anything! Additionally, while everyone should experience programs as directly as possible, it's imperative for your Go-Getters and Kindred Spirits. They need to feel it to believe it.

board dynamics

Here's a great story. When Andrea and I started Asking Matters, we tested the Asking Style Assessment with various organizations. One was a small university in upstate New York, which had its board take the assessment. After they were done Andrea and I were stunned—and deflated—by the results. Virtually the entire board scored as Mission Controllers, and we had to reach out to tell the director of development there was a glitch in the logarithms our test developer used.

Yet, when we shared this with the director, he said, "wow—you nailed it! That's exactly our challenge. We have tons of Mission Controllers on the board, and while we're happy to have them we can spend too much time in the details and we need a few people on the board to push big ideas."

As you can imagine, any group works better when a variety of perspectives and talents are represented. Rainmakers drive the group to go for the brass ring. Go-Getters passionately advocate for doing more and thinking outside the box. Kindred Spirits are the emotional arbiters, ensuring the organization understands its impact on various communities. And the Mission Controllers make sure those exciting and meaningful ideas are doable. They know that without a plan success is unlikely. As a board, this diversity enables them to fulfill their oversight and fiduciary responsibilities to the organization.

The extrovert/introvert balance of your board is also critical. The extroverted Rainmakers and Go-Getters are more likely to speak up in meetings and enjoy a healthy debate of ideas. The introverted Kindred Spirits and Mission Controllers will naturally say less at the time, wanting to share their thoughts later, and privately (remember they think to talk). Your job is to ensure everyone around the table speaks their mind in meetings so all perspectives are counted. Your board chair, through good leadership and understanding of group dynamics, can make sure this happens.

Once everyone on your board has taken the Asking Style Assessment (www.askingmatters.com/find-your-asking-style), you can review the results to better understand their strengths and challenges individually and as a team. You might notice holes in the overall board profile and request that your nominating committee looks for board members of particular Styles.

board positions

Further, your governing committee can use this information when placing board members on various committees. Your strategic planning committee needs at least a Rainmaker (strategy mindset) and Go-Getter (vision for the future), with a Mission Controller (systems) to ensure the planning is methodical and realistic. Of course, a Kindred Spirit (heart) will ensure your clients or participants voices are heard.

Your finance committee needs a number of analytics, though not to the exclusion of intuitives. The intuitives will make sure decisions are not only based on what is financially responsible; they'll push the committee to take some chances because it's the right thing to do.

Human Resources needs some Go-Getters and Kindred Spirits—intuitives who appreciate, and are sensitive to, personnel and personal dynamics. Mission Controllers will be sure the employee manual is complete, up-to-date, and implemented correctly. And Rainmakers will look at the policies from a strategic point of view relative to the organization's goals.

As you can see, every committee benefits from representation across the Asking Styles grid. Though it will generally be impossible to reach the ideal configuration across the board, if you look at committees through the Asking Styles lens you'll come much closer to having broad representation and perspective.

"Once they take the assessment, I say 'Oh, you are a so and so, and this person is also a ...' That makes them feel like they're in a group. Then I say, for example, 'Since you are a Mission Controller, you would be great at strengthening our case. You can poke holes in the case as you're looking for data and what hasn't been considered. Can I meet with you and have you help me in that regard?' Based on what they are, I give them assignments that are in their wheelhouses, and the language of the Styles becomes the shorthand for how we get volunteers involved and what we ask them to do."

—*Ninette R. Enrique, Director of Development,*
St. Luke's School, CT

fourteen

conclusion

the Asking Styles have had a profound effect on my life as a fundraiser, and I hope they will impact your life just as much.

Whereas before I thought I had to be something I wasn't—some ideal of an asker—now I proudly ask as a Kindred Spirit. I embrace all my great qualities as an asker and don't sweat the stuff I'm not. I turn down event invitations with confidence, as they're not the way I meet new prospects (or make new friends!). I talk from the heart and don't worry that I'm not using all the facts and figures.

I hope understanding the wonderful qualities of your Asking Style will give you the confidence to be yourself as an asker, as being yourself is the key to being a comfortable and successful asker. Never forget that fundraising is more about relationship building than anything else. Even in a meeting where you ask for a gift, building the relationship is most important. It may feel as if the gift is most important in that moment—your organization is counting on you to close the deal—but a strong relationship will lead to many gifts over many years.

To build a strong, lasting relationship you need to be your authentic self. You can't be something you think your donors want you to be, because your inauthenticity is guaranteed to show through...and it's so difficult to keep up the charade anyway! The best you is the real you. So embrace yourself for who you are.

Embrace yourself for all the wonderful qualities you have that make you a caring person who wants to help your organization have an impact and fulfill its vision for the world. For all the qualities your friends and family see in you that bring them close. For all the challenges that make you real.

Embrace your Rainmaker and go out to fundraise strategically, with all the facts and figures at the ready. Share your enthusiasm for outcomes measurements and demonstrate how your organization makes an impact through your "goal story." Never apologize for being competitive and driven to close the biggest gifts—we need you to do that!

Embrace your Go-Getter, drawing your donors in with endless enthusiasm and a deep belief that anything is possible. Go out to expand the circle by meeting new prospects and getting them excited about your organization. And don't sweat the details—there's someone who can help you stay on track and fill in the blanks!

Embrace your Kindred Spirit, and build lasting relationships through your selfless attention. Your heart comes through in everything you do, and that deep, emotional well is a great magnet to those around you. And if your conflict-averse nature keeps you from negotiating gifts as others might, know that you got further in the first place through the connections you built.

Embrace your Mission Controller, and knock it out of the park by listening to your donors. Take it slow and continue to be methodical and organized, never forgetting the turtle beat the hare! Some may want you to close a gift more quickly, but know when you do finally solicit that gift, your donor will be ready to come onboard.

Embrace who you are, and embrace—and appreciate—everyone else for the wonderful, special people they are. We all bring unique qualities to the art and science of asking...and no one has it all! Take the time to understand all the Asking Styles and to figure out the Styles of everyone on your team as well as those of your donors. Use that information to better understand all the personal dynamics of your working relationships and to fully appreciate everyone.

I'd like to close with a wonderful story from an Asking Styles fan:

"I'm a Kindred Spirit. Today I had to do a presentation to a local Rotary Club. We've been community partners with them for quite some time. They've given money for small projects here and there, and have put on small events for our clients. Today as I was preparing to give my talk I kept in mind that I'm a Kindred Spirit (with a splash of Go-Getter) and to embrace whatever comes out of my mouth. I asked them to give towards a room-renovation campaign that in truth we hadn't even begun yet, and they responded in droves! One man challenged the whole club to give $55 per person to help us reach an $8,000 goal for one room, and by the end of the meeting we had a cabinetmaker donating cabinets, and another man donating another $8,000 for a second room. In addition, when I got back to the office I had three emails from different members wanting to get involved. Everyone told me how moved they were by my presentation. It really made me think of what I learned from you and being a Kindred Spirit! So thanks for all you do!"

—Whitney Hughson, Director of Marketing
Susan B. Anthony Recovery Center, Pembroke Pines, FL

Go Whitney!

And "Go You!" to all the millions of you, professional and volunteer, who are out there asking for gifts. "Go You!" to the millions of you who get past the anxieties, the challenges, and the frustrations to do this difficult but important work—the work that enables your programs to impact countless lives.

Thank you for joining me in asking for gifts. Together we make the world a better place.

about the author

Brian Saber, president of Asking Matters™, has spent his entire career asking for money for nonprofits. From his early days as a student leader and telethon caller to his six years in charge of major and principal gifts throughout the Midwest for Brandeis University to his two stints as an executive director, every position has involved significant face-to-face solicitation. He is still honing his asking muscles today, cultivating and soliciting select major donors for a variety of clients.

Brian harnessed all his frontline experience to become a sought-after trainer, coach, and consultant around the country and abroad. His work is transformative. He leads workshops, creates training courses, presents webinars, and coaches top-level staff, taking organizations to the next level.

In a career spent mostly with organizations having budgets under $1 million, Brian is well aware of the fundraising challenges smaller organizations face. He knows most organizations struggle to afford consulting services; they're just not in the budget. With that perspective, Brian co-created Asking Matters to provide resources all nonprofits could afford. This web-based and in-person company trains people how to ask for money and motivates them to do it.

Brian has led training programs and presented at conferences for Prevent Child Abuse America, the Archdiocese of Los Angeles, Social Venture Partners International, National Public Radio, Volunteers of America, the U.S. Olympic Committee, The Salvation Army, Boys and Girls Clubs of America, AFP International, numerous AFP chapters, the North American YMCA Development Conference, and others.

Brian lives and works in South Orange, NJ. He is the proud father of a 17-year old son. In his spare time he attends the performing arts, volunteers for numerous organizations, practices yoga, and is immersed in singing lessons, which he started out of nowhere at the age of 54.

about asking matters™

Asking Matters was created by Andrea Kihlstedt & Brian Saber, two experienced fundraising professionals, who believed when it came to raising money, the primary limiting factor was people's reluctance to ask for gifts. Andrea, a capital campaign consultant, and Brian, a front-line fundraiser and consultant, decided to develop a set of practical, accessible tools to help staff and board members learn the art and science of asking and find the courage and will to ask.

Through her work on capital campaigns, Andrea knew that when the stakes were high enough to get people to ask, the results were remarkable, with organizations often raising far more money than anyone thought possible. And Brian, a front-line fundraiser who has asked thousands of people for hundreds of millions of dollars of gifts, knew it was possible to overcome one's fears and ask...and ask and ask. He believed that, while it might never get easy and often isn't fun, the results were well worth the discomfort and often yield much more than money.

In 2009, Andrea and Brian launched Asking Matters, a company that uses web-based learning and in-person training to provide the information and inspiration needed to motivate staff and board members to ask. In 2013 Brian acquired Andrea's share, and he continues to own and run the company today.

acknowledgments

Andrea Kihlstedt is a rock star and I owe so much to her. There would be no Asking Matters without her, just as there would be no Asking Styles without her. The original ideas for what became the Asking Styles were hers, and I am forever grateful that she partnered with me to develop them and then entrusted their future to me. Andrea's been a steadfast friend and peer, and her generosity is unparalleled.

Many thanks to Stephen Nill of CharityChannel Press. Steve published Andrea's original book on the Asking Styles back in 2013, and it is only through his generosity (along with Andrea's) that this book will now be the Asking Styles primer for our field. He has my lifelong appreciation.

I owe so much to my entire Asking Matters team. They've been steadfast in their loyalty, creative and dedicated in their work, and generous and thoughtful in their advice. First to my editors: Jodi Chromey, Sue Kindred, Larry Greenberg and Thomas West. It's amazing how much editors bring to bear on the final product. Special thanks to Tom West for all his additional work designing this book and getting it published. I can't imagine this book without his help.

Thank you to everyone who agreed to be quoted or referenced in the book. Your voices have brought the material alive. Special thanks to Jerry Panas, who generously agreed to write the foreword, and to Whitney Hughson, Ron Manderschied, Lisa Metcalf, and Judi Smith, whose stories are so empowering.

Thanks to the rest of the Asking Matters team for all their behind-the-scenes work: Michele Ericson-Stern, Kevin Gaertner, Anna Veronica Gargarita, Kyle Nunes & Gary Ziffer. And thanks to my Asking Matters Experts: Michael Davidson, Andrea Kihlstedt, Sue Kindred and Joe Tumolo. I've learned so much from their expertise and cherish their collegiality.

Last but not least, I acknowledge my son, Richard. He is my world.

—Brian

Made in the
USA
Monee, IL